£16.95

Handbook
of Group Activities
for Impaired
Older Adults

About the Authors

Elsbeth Martindale Helgeson—is a licensed Marriage, Family, and Child Counselor who is presently completing her Doctorate in Clinical Psychology at Rosemead Graduate School of Psychology. Ms. Helgeson created many of the activities for this handbook while completing a psychology internship at the Community Assistance Program for Seniors (CAPS) in Pasadena, California. She is currently working part-time as an M.F.C.C. while also working on the completion of her doctoral dissertation.

Scott Cabot Willis—is a doctoral candidate in clinical psychology at the Graduate School of Psychology, Fuller Theological Seminary. He has worked in the field of Gerontology for a number of years and is presently a Director of Group Activities at the Community Assistance Program for Seniors, a day care/day treatment center for people with Alzheimer's Disease, Parkinson's Disease, and other similar illnesses.

Handbook of Group Activities for Impaired Older Adults

Elsbeth Martindale Helgeson
Scott Cabot Willis

The Haworth Press
New York • London

Handbook of Group Activities for Impaired Older Adults has also been published as *Activities, Adaptation & Aging*, Volume 9, Number 2, Winter 1986.

The Haworth Press, Inc., 12 West 32 Street, New York, NY 10001
EUROSPAN/Haworth, 3 Henrietta Street, London WC2E 8LU England

Library of Congress Cataloging-in-Publication Data

Helgeson, Elsbeth Martindale.

Handbook of group activities for impaired older adults.

"Has also been published as Activities, adaptation & aging, volume 9, number 2, winter 1986" – T.p. verso.
1. Occupational therapy for the aged – Handbook, manuals, etc. 2. Small groups – Handbooks, manuals, etc. 3. Aged – Rehabilitation – Handbooks, manuals, etc. I. Willis, Scott Cabot. II. Title.
RC953.8.022H44   1987   616.8'046515   87-274
ISBN 0-86656-628-7

Handbook of Group Activities
for Impaired Older Adults

Activities, Adaptation & Aging
Volume 9, Number 2

CONTENTS

Foreword

Gerontology is a new and rapidly growing discipline. As with any young field of study, it is only beginning to develop its own body of research and unique set of literature. The psychological and social needs of the elderly are vast. Much is needed in terms of empirical research and clinical literature in this area. Helgeson and Willis have added an important and significant volume to this growing body of literature and a number of its features should be highlighted.

The Community Assistance Program for Seniors (CAPS) is one of four gerontology programs operated by The Psychological Center. The Psychological Center is composed of twelve programs and is the arm of action for the Graduate School of Psychology at Fuller Theological Seminary. Each of our clinical programs must provide a high level of training for our students and, at the same time, render a high quality of service to the community while supporting programmatic research. The CAPS program is a training facility for graduate students in clinical and community gerontology and, no less importantly, a day care and day treatment facility for victims of Alzheimer's Disease and related disorders. In this setting, the *Handbook of Group Activities for Impaired Older Adults* has proved itself to be an asset to the clients and staff of the CAPS program.

The clients served at the CAPS program are those in the later stages of Alzheimer's Disease or are severely disabled in some other way. These individuals have become an extremely burdensome caretaking responsibility for their families. The activities contained in this manual provide the foundation for a daily program that becomes therapy for the participants and respite for their families. The activities are creatively designed and well organized to help enable these clients to obtain as much human interaction and achieve as much of a sense of self-worth as is possible within their tremendous limitations. The families, which are often composed of a single caretaker, are given respite and allowed a reprieve from the high level of stress they experience. Often, family members will come into the program and observe the clients engaged in one of these activities and will come away with a new sense of hope and the reassurance that the one they love is well cared for.

Since this handbook has come into being, the staff has had a valuable resource designed specifically for this population. There are very few books available that focus upon activity ideas for adults with severe deficits. Planning and organizing the program around these activities has helped to achieve stability and consistency in our treatment. This handbook has also been a vital addition to the training materials used in our clinic. Sections like "Guidelines for Leading a Group Activity" and "Philosophy of Treatment" help our students to enhance their clinical skills and to develop a rationale for treatment.

Helgeson and Willis have created a practical and effective book that fills an important vacancy in clinical gerontology. Psychologists, psychiatrists, social workers, recreational therapists, and group therapists will find this handbook easy to use and flexible enough to be applicable in a wide range of settings where severely impaired adults are gathered.

Paul W. Clement, PhD
Director
The Psychological Center
Graduate School of Psychology
Fuller Theological Seminary

Preface

This workbook is a result of our frustrations and joys in working with impaired older adults. The frustration came as we looked for activities to do at the day treatment center where we worked and found virtually nothing published on the practical how-to level of designing therapeutic group activities. Our joy came out of creation and experimentation of activities that were stimulating and therapeutic. We decided we should compile these and allow others to see what we had come up with so they too can create activities that are suitable for their program. So here it is!

We want to dedicate this book to all the members of the day treatment program who were patient with us as we tried out our ideas, stumbled and triumphed. We also want to thank the staff at the Community Assistance Program for Seniors especially Jim Otteson, Bobbi Norton, and Bruce Atkinson for sharing their ideas and providing encouragement.

INTRODUCTION

This handbook is designed to be a practical resource and guide for those persons who prepare and lead group activities for impaired older adults. Those working in nursing or convalescent hospitals, day care or day treatment facilities, and retirement homes will find this handbook especially useful. When we began to lead groups of moderately to severely impaired older adults, we discovered that there was virtually no published literature on activities designed for use with this population. We tried to use activities designed for children, adolescents, and young adults, but found these to be grossly inadequate for an impaired older population. We thus created our own ideas based on modifications of what we have read and our own ingenuity. We have learned a great deal by doing this and we came up with some excellent activities that are enjoyable and therapeutic.

The activities in this book are written in a manner that we hope will be easy to use. At the top of many activity listings is a picture of a piece of cake. This is to indicate the activity described is very simple to utilize and can be used with practically no preparation. Each activity is also rated with symbols according to its main therapeutic value (the key for these symbols is located on page 7). We have categorized the activities according to their potential to facilitate emotional expression, enhance problem solving skills, stimulate one or more of the sensory systems, and encourage social interaction. The headings marked, "Group Size," "Time Involved," "Materials Needed," "Description/Directions," and "Guidelines for Adaptation," give necessary information for conducting the group activities. Be sure to read thoroughly the section on "Guidelines for Adaptation". This section contains valuable information that will be helpful in tailoring the activities to the needs of your particular group. You may use the remaining space on each page for your own helpful "Notes."

We have included additional information in this book that we believe may be helpful. We have defined what we mean by "impaired" and have given you a description of our philosophy of treatment. We have presented helpful guidelines for leading groups with impaired adults and have discussed the structure of the groups themselves. Also included is a schedule for a typical day of activities. We challenge you to read these sections and try the principles suggested, as we have found them highly effective in working with impaired older adults. At the end of the book there is a section on working with crafts which is intended to help you understand the special problems associated with using crafts in a treatment setting. Also, we have included some crafts ideas we found useful and enjoyable in our setting. Additionally, we have included a section on ways in which you can generate your own activities. This section is designed to help you create activities that are enjoyable and unique to your particular group.

We hope that your involvement with challenging older adults is enhanced by this workbook.

What Do We Mean by "Impaired?"

Handbook of Group Activities for Impaired Older Adults is indeed a long title. Perhaps the one part of this title that is unclear is the meaning of the word impaired. Specifically, when we talk of "impaired" we are referring to any person who is suffering from a significant physical, emotional, or mental loss of ability to function normally. A wide variety of diseases, disorders, and conditions fit into this category, including persons diagnosed as having Organic Brain Syndrome, Alzheimer's Disease, various dementias, Parkinson's Disease, Korsakoff's Disease, amnestic syndromes, strokes, head traumas, tumors, depression, deafness, and blindness. These older adults, who fit into the above categories, are those with whom we have worked and for whom these activities have been developed. We are not saying that individuals must fit into one or more of the above categories in order for this book to be useful. The extent to which this book can be utilized with various groups can only be realized by those of you who are willing to "give it a try."

Also implied, but not stated directly, is the assumption that "impaired older adults" means moderately to severely impaired. Individuals who are mildly impaired can still benefit from most of the available activities for senior citizens in general, such as community centers, recreational and tour groups, and mental health services. It is only when a person becomes more severely impaired or difficult to care for that they find their way into a day treatment clinic, day care center, residential home, or a nursing/convalescent hospital. Treating these individuals in groups is often the most economical means of service for these institutions. This handbook can help to make these groups of severely impaired adults an entertaining, enjoyable, effective, and therapeutic enterprise.

Philosophy of Treatment

We believe this activity book will prove to be of greater use to you and your staff if we take some time to explain our philosophy concerning treatment of impaired older adults.

The activities in this book are a result of hundreds of hours of group work with moderately to severely impaired adults in a Day Care/Day Treatment facility. Directing group activities in this, or a similar setting, can be challenging for several reasons. First of all, the range of functioning of the participants will be skewed towards the end of the continuum which includes the severely impaired. Persons with mild impairment or those in the early stages of dementia generally continue to function fairly well in their normal setting and usually do not show up in nursing homes or day care settings until they become more severely impaired.

A second factor is that a group of impaired older clients will show tremendous individual variability in terms of progression of the diseases and skills or abilities retained and lost. Add to this the likelihood of other physical or emotional disabilities and the result is a group in which a great many factors will need to be considered when planning an activity. Thus, the group leader becomes one of the most important elements in the success of group activities for impaired older adults. The leader, we believe, must be **perceptive** in order to take notice of problems and discomfort at both the individual and group level. The leader must be **empathic**, in order to sense *and* communicate an understanding and concern for the needs of each individual. It is also important for the leader to be **flexible** and able to make spontaneous changes. It is often important to modify activities to make them meaningful for the group as a whole while also considering the unique needs of each individual participant.

We would like to discuss what we consider to be a successful group experience. Underlying all the activities presented in this handbook are four basic goals that we strive to achieve. We consider these to be essential elements of a therapeutic experience for impaired clients whether it be in a group milieu or in a one on one situation. First and foremost, we **affirm each participant as a person and give them all the rights and respect of a human being**. This simple attitude can be of great benefit to the impaired adult who may have lost their sense of pride and self respect. This attitude of respect may be absent among spouses, children, family members, or caretakers who have watched their loved one slowly lose their abilities and have reacted to this with frustration, impatience, and anger. Our goal is to affirm these individuals in spite of their deficits and help them to find new ways to esteem themselves.

A second goal is to **challenge each client within their limits so that they can achieve a sense of mastery and accomplishment**. It is very difficult to assess just how much some severely impaired clients can understand and perceive. However, we believe that the need to actualize one's potential is intrinsic to each and every human being regardless of their level of impairment. A feature then, in utilizing each activity, is for the group leader to insure that the activity challenges each client in the upper ranges of his or her abilities without producing undue frustration. Simply put, the group leader must know the group members in terms of their level of functioning and their remaining abilities. Each activity in this handbook has a sub-section entitled "Guidelines for Adaptation." The group leader should be familiar with these sections so that s/he can spontaneously adjust the activity to meet the differing needs of the participants and to challenge them appropriately. By utilizing the activities in this manner, each client will be able to gain a sense of accomplishment, success, and mastery in the presented task. This will yield feelings of comfort, support, security, and acceptance.

A third goal is to **help each client make a healthy adjustment to their impairment**. This is probably the most difficult of our four goals since it depends a great deal on each person's premorbid personality and coping abilities. It is not entirely clear to us whether or not memory impaired adults, as a whole, can learn new coping skills. Our experience indicates that some can, and do, while others have great difficulty accepting their condition and adopt an angry or helpless posture. Our goal is to elicit coping and problem solving skills, to help the clients recognize these, and learn to transfer them to other areas of their lives if possible. The more they can utilize the remaining skills and abilities they have, the better their chances for making a healthy adjustment to their impairment.

Our final goal is to **reverse the process of isolation and withdrawal that tends to occur and help clients become connected with and concerned for other group members and staff**. Probably more than 80% of the clients we have worked with have, as a treatment goal, some form of increase in socialization and contact with others. Mere contact with others in the group milieu will facilitate this process, but specific attention to this need is also important. Each activity included in this handbook has been positively evaluated for its ability to encourage interaction. Many activities encourage the sharing of personal information, while others encourage working together as a team. Both of these functions increase interaction and engagement with others. The group leader and the support staff can do much to develop and encourage relationships with other clients and with the staff.

We have used symbols to code the various activities in terms of the "therapeutic value" of each activity. Classifying the activities in this manner has helped us to decide what kind of activity may be useful for a particular group depending upon our goals and the needs of the group. Several symbols may appear together on one description, indicating rich therapeutic value for that activity. Also, please note that the therapeutic value of each activity may exceed what has been indicated. The symbol simply indicates the most obvious therapeutic enhancement.

Key to Symbols

This symbol indicates the activity is "a piece of cake" for the group leader to prepare and implement. The activity will not require external preparation if all the materials in the "materials needed" section are available. Look for this symbol when you need an activity in a hurry!

Indicates an activity that facilitates emotional expression.

Indicates an activity that enhances problem solving skills.

Indicates an activity that stimulates one or more of the sensory systems.

Indicates an activity that encourages social interaction.

Guidelines for Leading a Group Activity

Leading group activities with impaired older adults can be a very rewarding experience. Many of these individuals do not get the attention and care they desire. Having an attitude of love and acceptance no matter what deficits are encountered generally yields a warm and engaging response. Experiencing the opportunity to touch someone who is hungry for affection, or to hear someone who often feels ignored, is very satisfying to both parties involved.

Leading a group activity with impaired adults can also be a very trying experience. It may be very difficult to get and keep the participant's attention. Group members may decide to wander or begin talking with their neighbor in the middle of a prepared activity, which of course disrupts the group's involvement. The leader must be vigilant to insure that the hard of hearing have the best possible opportunity to hear and those who are losing their sight are in the best possible position for seeing. The leader must try to balance the needs of the lower functioning persons with those of the higher functioning members. When memory problems are a feature of some of the group members, the leader may need to repeat instructions often and reorient participants to the present social reality (i.e., their participation in a group). Having strong support staff is essential, especially in groups where the level of functioning varies significantly. When the staff is in unison and working together the atmosphere will reflect this, leading to a sense of security among the clients. Again, the group leader is one of the most important elements in turning any of these activities into a great activity!

It works best to have one person designated as the leader. However, the entire staff must always work together as a team. A team does not function very well without a coach, manager, quarterback, captain or other type of leader. It is far too confusing, for both the group members as well as the staff, to participate in a group without a specified leader who can provide direction and maintain a central focus.

In our work with impaired adults, we have discovered several important factors we would like to propose as guidelines. These guidelines help the activities run smooth and become rewarding to both the clients and the staff. They are as follows:

1. **Avoid infantilizing the participants.** Although some of the individuals may talk like infants, wear diapers, and may need to be fed, they are fully developed as persons. They may have lost some of their ability to function as normal adults but they have not lost their personhood. They are human beings and must be respected as such.

2. **Be patient.** Give each member time to respond. Encourage clients to use as much of their skills as they can without becoming overly frustrated. When questions are asked to clients, allow them to generate as much of the answer as they can before giving them support. Give clues before you give answers. Self expression is of highest value and it is important to encourage the participants to express themselves.

3. **Be observant.** Everybody is different and unique. Take an interest in each person and note their preferences, personality style, and individual characteristics. Comment on these, allowing them to feel their own special place in the group. Impairments in older adults can be manifested in a myriad of ways and no two members will be alike in personality or in the use of their remaining abilities. Knowing the clients as individuals is important. Watch closely for signs of distress and discomfort and respond to these as

quickly as possible. Again, having observant, supportive, and trained staff is essential.

4. **Be flexible.** It is very important to be able to make spontaneous changes while the activity continues. You may need to change the tempo, level of difficulty, eliminate distractions, retrieve their attention, or incorporate peripheral members into the flow of the activity. Occasionally, the group activity may escalate into a state of chaos, or an emergency will occur, such that you will need to stop the activity altogether and make immediate changes. If any activity does not seem to be working properly, do not hesitate to discard it and go on to something else.

5. **Keep a central focus.** Generally the group leader will be the center of focus. S/he may want to stand up and speak loudly in order to be heard and seen by the group members. Having the participants sit in a circle or semicircle allows each of the members to see the leader and all the other group members. When a group member is talking, it may be helpful for the group leader to go and stand beside this individual to make it easier for the other members to track with who is speaking. Try to avoid having staff or assistants participate from outside of the group circle, as this distracts the group and limits the use of staff as models. Minimize any distractions that occur outside the circle. An amplifier and microphone are valuable tools that allow the hard of hearing to participate more fully.

6. **Give as much input to the different sensory modalities as possible.** This will help most individuals get a fuller impact of any message. When addressing someone give them a light touch or gently stroke their arm. When giving instructions for an activity or task, say it , write it down (e.g., on a chalkboard), and demonstrate it. This allows individuals to use their skills in different sensory areas and allows them to combine these skills if necessary

in order to understand the task more completely. Modeling is one of the most important aspects of leading any activity. Even if participants cannot understand the rules, or forget what is to be done, they can observe others and participate by imitating their actions.

7. **Help construct social reality.** Day dreaming, memory impairment, and loss of attention will cause a participant to forget where s/he is at. This may result in anxiety, emotional outbursts, wandering, and a host of other behaviors. Therefore, it is often necessary to reconstruct social reality for them. This means refocusing their attention to the group and upon the present activity. If participants disregard social rules it is likely they have forgotten where they are and who they are with. Gently reminding them that they are in a group will usually prompt conformity to the social norms. Again, gentleness is important. Try not to embarrass these persons, but to encourage a sense of acceptance and pride in who they are.

8. **Give attention to strengths.** Many of the clients that come to group treatment programs are highly aware of their impairments. These are persons who are struggling to maintain a sense of self-worth in the face of tremendous physical, cognitive, and emotional losses. It is helpful to focus on remaining abilities and strengths rather than on the deficits. Clients will begin to feel better about themselves and have higher self-esteem when others give attention to their strengths. The pain and discomfort of these individuals should not be neglected, but as much as possible present activities that emphasize the individual's remaining strengths and avoid activities that leave people feeling discouraged and defeated. This book has been assembled with that purpose in mind. Be liberal with compliments, warmth, respect, and touch.

Types of Group Activities

Group activities can be broken down into several different types. It is important to employ various types of activities at different times during the day. The first type is **focusing activities**. The purpose of these activities are to bring the group together and to make everyone feel like they are a part of the whole group. Addressing each individual in the group and commenting on their presence and importance to the group is the primary goal of a focusing activity. Focusing activities are important at both the beginning and end of each day. In the beginning of the day, these activities orient individuals and help to make them feel they belong in the group. At the end of the day, focusing activities allow time for closure and a recap of the day's events.

Focusing activities are also helpful to use when the group appears fragmented and disoriented during the day. Momentarily suspending the activity at hand and reminding the group of where they are in the daily schedule and of the present task can be a helpful exercise. Sometimes it may be necessary to completely drop the present activity and change to a more intense focusing activity in order to reorient a distracted group. A relaxation or guided imagery activity may be advised because of the stilling and calming effect it can have on the group. Other activities we have used as focusing activities are Attending to Feelings, Expressing Thankfulness, Fairy Tales, Friendship Squeeze, Hush and Listen, Origin of a Name, Personal Concerns, and Sharing Caring.

Stimulator activities are activities that are intended to provide physical stimulation or to wake up a sleepy group. They involve physical movement of either short or long duration. Exercises, backrubs, handrubs, songs, walks, outdoor games, or other physically stimulating actions are examples of stimulator activities. Most of the activities marked with the symbol for sensory stimulation will fit this category.

Filler activities are short activities that can be used to fill in a spare five to fifteen minutes. Check the "time involved" area on each activity page to see if the activity could be done in the amount of time available. We found that chaining several filler activities together becomes distracting and confusing to the clients. Fillers are best used before or after a major activity rather than as a series to fill up a longer period of time. Both focusing activities and stimulator activities can make excellent fillers.

Major activities are activities that last from twenty minutes to one hour. All of the activities listed in this book are designed to be completed in an hour or less, although some of them are easily extended to ninety minutes. Going beyond an hour without at least a brief break or change of pace is often too much for impaired older adults. If activities go beyond an hour be sure that each of the participants are frequently addressed and asked to participate. It is also important to consider the need for breaks in a long program, for toileting and meeting other essential needs.

Major activities can be conducted in a large group or in smaller subgroups. Cooking, for example, is an activity we chose to do as a group activity for "women only." We had this group once a week during which time the men were involved in a different activity for "men only." Each of the activities listed in this workbook are marked as to the preferred group size. The large group can be broken in to smaller groups of persons with similar impairments or levels of functioning.

Additionally, **specialized activities** such as group therapy, family therapy, recreational therapy, physical rehabilitation, and education groups are beneficial additions to your program. Of course, most of these activities will need to be conducted by an individual with training in the specialized area. The type of clientele you service will determine which type of specialized activities, if any, will be appropriate for you to incorporate.

Schedule for a Typical Day

Below is a general schedule that we use to program a whole day of group activities at the day treatment center where we work. We found that one major activity in the morning and one in the afternoon was preferable. Again, in doing these longer activities there is a constant need to monitor the group's attention and to make sure the majority are interested and participating in the activity. Those that tend to lose concentration need to be addressed frequently and encouraged to participate when appropriate.

Morning

Greetings/Socializing time

It may be helpful to have this time fairly unstructured in the beginning while clients arrive and join the group. A friendly handshake or other type of physical contact will help to make each person feel welcome.

Focusing Activity

The purpose of this activity is to orient everyone to the group. Make sure to address everyone and engage them in some fashion.

Present the day's schedule

Writing this out on a chalkboard may be helpful.

Reality orientation activities may also be appropriate.

Major Activity or Specialized Activity

Stimulator Activity

Filler Activity (optional)

Lunch

Allow for socializing after the meal.

Afternoon

Focusing Activity

Stimulator Activity

This is especially helpful after lunch when people tend to get drowsy.

Major Activity

Focusing Activity

This focusing activity should help orient the clients to the fact that the day at the center is almost over. Going over the activities they participated in during the day may be a useful way to close.

This last part of the day is usually the most difficult because of the disruption of people leaving the program and other clients becoming restless.

Dividing the group into smaller groups depending on the time they leave the program will help to lessen the distraction.

Goodbyes

Remind clients of when they will be back to the program. Giving them a note to remind them of this may be helpful with those individuals whose memories are failing.

Planning Group Activities

In planning for a day of group activities, several concerns need to be addressed. First, an **elimination of distractions** is essential toward helping the group members maintain a focus upon the group activity. Staff and/or clients who are constantly coming in or going out of the group room become disruptive to the group and lead to frustration. Some clients have difficulty concentrating to begin with and constant movement and change makes it even more difficult to attend to the group activity. Some settings are not conducive to the needs of these clients. Outside noise (i.e., children playing, sirens, street traffic, etc.) may make it difficult for some to concentrate. Inside noise (i.e., heaters, air conditioners, telephones, etc.) can also be a disturbing factor. Having a view of outside activity through windows or doors may cause some members to loose their concentration. Being aware of these issues and planning to avoid as many distractions as possible will aid in the smooth functioning of all group activities.

A second essential element is the importance of **considering the various needs** of each of the participants. Some individuals will have short attention spans, some will have physical concerns that necessitate physical adjustment and mobility, while others will be content and may even prefer to sit silently for hours. It is difficult to satisfy everyone's wishes, but being aware of the differing needs will be the first step in attempting to make everyone feel as comfortable as possible. We found that having a record available of each individual's physical, emotional, and social needs is helpful to the staff in preparing and implementing activities. This record needs to be continually updated so the staff can keep on top of difficulties and changes as they arise.

A third important ingredient to planning a whole day of successful group activities is the **availability of alternative activities**. The reason for writing a book such as this is to give group leaders alternatives to group programing and to have these alternatives organized, practical, and easily accessible. The needs of the group will vary and their interest in activities will change. You may discover, as we have, that a particular activity will create a therapeutic environment and be a lot of fun on one day and the next time you try it, turn out to be a disaster. A whole host of factors may cause this turn-around. If the cause is readily discernable, such as a disruptive client or lack of support staff, then the leader is responsible to act quickly to remedy the problem. However, as is often the case, it will not be clear why a particular activity does not achieve what you want it to. Thus, allowing for flexibility and being able to make spontaneous modifications is essential to planning and implementing a program of effective group activities. Periodically re-reading the guidelines for adaptation section of those activities you use frequently may reveal variations that can add to your repertoire of available alternative activities.

One of the tasks that continually confronts the group leader is to monitor the needs of the clients. We cannot emphasize this enough. Observing the verbal and non-verbal behavior of the clients while you are leading the group will be your best indicator as to whether you need to change to another activity or to modify the present activity. If you find this to be too challenging while leading the activity, you will want to instruct your support staff to be observant of the group members and to give you feedback as the activity progresses.

You may also find that the needs of a particular member do not mesh well with the rest of the group. Once again, it is vitally important to be aware of special circumstances and to have alternative activities for individuals who find participation in a particular group activity to be difficult. Ideally, there should be a room available where individuals are free to go when they are not willing to be involved in the group. Activities available for such individuals should encompass a wide range of functioning levels. Materials for journaling, small crafts, music and headphones, individual games (i.e., word puzzles, jigsaw puzzles, playing cards, etc.) and books or magazines to read, are useful with higher functioning individuals. Lower functioning individuals will be likely to need more supervision, but simple materials are often all that is needed. Creativity is necessary in these situations. Placing yourself in the shoes of the impaired individual is a useful strategy in arriving at an acceptable alternative. You might ask, "If I were Mrs. Smith in this situation, what would make me feel comfortable and involved?" One woman we worked with was a compulsive "cleaner-upper" as well as someone who consistently disrupted the group. Given the task of sorting out peas and beans from macaroni gave her a project that kept her concentrated and content while the group maintained an uninterrupted activity.

On Hand Materials

Below is a list of materials that we found helpful to keep on hand. The majority of the activities in this book can be done if the following materials are on hand in your program room:

construction paper

scissors

magazines (to be cut up)

glue sticks (these seem to work better than glue in a bottle)

colored pens, crayons, and felt markers

pens and pencils

plain paper

beach ball

large rubber or plastic ball (12-18 inch)

balloons

tape recorder/player

ACTIVITIES

ACTORS AND ACTRESSES

THERAPEUTIC VALUE:

GROUP SIZE: Any size
TIME INVOLVED: 10-45 minutes
MATERIALS NEEDED: none
DESCRIPTION/DIRECTIONS: Individuals volunteer to act in one of the
following categories without using words:
1) **emotions** - rage, despair, hope, fear, misery, happiness, infatuation, joy,
jealousy, peace, sorrow, pride, inferiority, suspicion, frustration, etc..
2) **trades** - truck driver, ditch digger, bus driver, lumberjack, violinist, painter,
school teacher, cook, farmer, athlete, auto mechanic, etc..
3) **sensations** - hunger, howling wind, quiet stream, soft whisper, angry storm,
crashing waves, happy memory, bad dream, gentle rain, fog creeping in,
beautiful flower, creaking door, tumbling leaves, falling snowflake, slithering
snake, etc..
The players are given their acting task secretly (i.e., written on paper or
whispered in ear) and others can guess what they are depicting. It may be
helpful to stay within one category of acting options so as to limit confusion.
GUIDELINES FOR ADAPTATION:
If it is difficult for the group members to participate in acting, the staff
may choose to act while the group guesses. For *lower functioning*
individuals a list of options for guessing may be written on a chalkboard.
Higher functioning individuals may choose a gesture on their own, if they
prefer. Gestures do not necessarily need to fall into one of the above
categories.

NOTES:

ATTENDING TO FEELINGS

THERAPEUTIC VALUE:

☺ ?

GROUP SIZE: Any size
TIME INVOLVED: 10-60 minutes
MATERIALS NEEDED: Feeling list (see next page) and chalkboard (possibly magazines)
DESCRIPTION/DIRECTIONS: Feelings may be explored in many ways. Several ideas are listed below:
1) List three feelings that are somewhat similar in nature (e.g., happy, joyful, elated). Discuss the differences in the three feelings. Ask for examples of when these feelings were felt.
2) Write a feeling word on the board and discuss its meaning. Ask for examples of when someone has felt that feeling or ask someone to make up a story involving that emotion.
3) Draw a "feeling face" on the chalkboard, in simple form, that depicts the expression of a feeling. Several can be drawn at once and the description of the affect could be listed below, making the task a matching one. Have group members identify the feelings and discuss it. The discussion can include when they may have felt this in the past or what thoughts are associated with the feeling. (An excellent poster titled "How Do You Feel Today?" is a useful tool for drawing faces.)
4) Ask individual group members to nonverbally depict certain feelings using facial expressions or other nonverbal forms of communication.
5) Cut pictures from magazines (or other sources) depicting human faces expressing various emotions. Discuss the feelings portrayed in each picture. Ask members to tell a story about what they think might have happened to make the person feel the way they do. Ask for examples of times when group members have felt similar feelings.
6) In small groups look through magazines for pictures to express specific feelings. Cut out the pictures and make posters.
GUIDELINES FOR ADAPTATION:
   Lower functioning individuals may have more success on the last three ideas listed above. With the absence of verbal skills, activities that involve looking and pointing may be more suitable. By having "feeling faces" on cards or glued to popsicle sticks, you may allow them to pick the face that depicts the feeling they may want to express.
NOTES:

FEELING LIST

abandoned	fearful	negative	sexy
affectionate	foolish	nervous	shocked
ambivalent	frustrated	nice	silly
angry	frightened	noble	skeptical
annoyed	free	obnoxious	sneaky
anxious	gay	obsessed	solemn
apathetic	glad	odd	sorrowful
awed	gratified	optimistic	spiteful
bad	greedy	opposed	startled
betrayed	grief	outraged	stingy
bitter	guilty	overjoyed	stuffed
blue	happy	overwhelmed	stunned
bold	hateful	pain	stupid
bored	homesick	panic	suffering
brave	horrible	peaceful	sure
bubbly	hurt	persecuted	sympathetic
burdened	ignored	petrified	talkative
calm	impressed	pity	tense
capable	infatuated	pleasant	tentative
challenged	inspired	pleased	terrible
cheated	isolated	precarious	terrified
cheerful	jealous	pressured	threatened
childish	joyous	pretty	tired
competitive	jubilant	proud	trapped
confused	jumpy	qualified	troubled
content	kind	quarrelsome	ugly
crushed	kinky	queasy	uneasy
defeated	lazy	queer	unlimited
delighted	left out	quiet	unsettled
despair	lonely	rage	uplifted
determined	longing	refreshed	useful
distracted	loving	rejected	vain
disturbed	low	relaxed	valiant
dominated	lustful	relieved	violent
dynamite	mad	remorse	vital
eager	magnificent	restless	venturesome
ecstatic	marvelous	reverent	vulnerable
empty	mean	rewarded	wicked
energetic	melancholy	righteous	wonderful
envious	miserable	sad	weepy
excited	mystical	satisfied	worry
exhausted	naughty	scared	zany
fascinated	needed	settled	zealous

BALLOON VOLLEYBALL

THERAPEUTIC VALUE:

GROUP SIZE: Two teams of 6-18 persons
TIME INVOLVED: 15-45 minutes
MATERIALS NEEDED: Balloons (large round)
DESCRIPTION/DIRECTIONS: This is an excellent activity for individuals at all levels of impairment. Line up two rows of chairs facing each other. The rows should be fairly close to each other, three to four feet apart. Participants sit in the chairs and attempt to hit a balloon over the heads of the opposing team. Assistants need to stand behind each of the rows to retrieve the balloon.

GUIDELINES FOR ADAPTATION:

For *lower functioning* individuals the task may be to just keep the balloon from dropping to the ground rather than hitting it over the heads of the opposite team.

For *large groups* two balloons may be used at once to keep things more stimulating.

NOTES:

BIRTHDAY CELEBRATIONS

THERAPEUTIC VALUE:

GROUP SIZE: Any size
TIME INVOLVED: 10-60 minutes
MATERIALS NEEDED: none (construction paper for cards and hats)
DESCRIPTION/DIRECTIONS: Birthdays are a special time for all of us. People usually enjoy having their birthday recognized. There are several ways to make birthdays special in a group of impaired older adults.

Singing is common on birthdays, as we all know. The singing can be enhanced with rhythm instruments that are purchased or made (i.e. paper plates stapled together with dried peas, beans or rice inside).

Birthday cards can be made by using construction paper and pictures from magazines. The pictures can be of something pretty and decorative or could be pictures of gifts that they would like to buy for the person celebrating their birthday.

Making birthday hats can also be fun and add to the festivity. These can be made by folding a rectangular piece of paper into a cone shape, stapling it together, and decorating it with glitter, stickers, and yarn.

GUIDELINES FOR ADAPTATION:

High functioning individuals may wish to share memories of special birthdays they remember. Feelings about getting older can be discussed.

All clients and especially *lower functioning* individuals may enjoy the touch of others as a special birthday gift. Backrubs, neckrubs, hand massages make excellent gifts. The group members can be encouraged to offer such gifts to the person celebrating their birthday.

NOTES:

CATEGORY LISTING

THERAPEUTIC VALUE:

GROUP SIZE: Small groups in competition (adapt to large group)
TIME INVOLVED: 15-45 minutes
MATERIALS NEEDED: Paper and pencil
DESCRIPTION/DIRECTIONS: Participants sit in groups of four to six, each group
is given a piece of paper. An individual with writing ability is designated for
each group (may be staff). All groups are given the same category (or
categories) to mark on their paper (i.e., vegetables, fruits, automobiles, Bible
characters, books, actors, musical instruments, bodies of water, things smaller
than 5 inches, things found in kitchens, etc.). The leader calls out a letter of
the alphabet and each group is given several minutes in which to list words
beginning with that letter under each category. The team with the most
entries wins.
GUIDELINES FOR ADAPTATION:
   It may be more useful for the leader to give each team a different letter of
the alphabet so that the teams may shout out responses in their groups
without fearing being overheard and thus giving away an answer. These
letters can then be rotated among the groups so that lists can be compared
equally.
   Giving each team a card on which the designated letter is printed boldly
may help the participants to stay more focused on the task.
   Categories may be disregarded altogether and participants asked to list all
items they can think of that begin with a particular letter of the alphabet. A
time limit of 30 seconds may be appropriate.
A letter of the alphabet may be disregarded altogether and participants may be
asked to list as many items as they can think of from any particular category.
   One large group - the leader can list the categories on a chalkboard and the
group as a whole can generate the appropriate lists.
   Higher functioning individuals can compete as individuals or in pairs.

NOTES:

COOKING

THERAPEUTIC VALUE:

GROUP SIZE: Small group no larger than 15

TIME INVOLVED: 45-90 minutes

MATERIALS NEEDED: A recipe and all the ingredients called for, cooking utensils and bowls, an oven or stove

DESCRIPTION/DIRECTIONS: Many different things can be made as a group. Those products that involve a number of steps that would include the participation of many members are preferred. For example, you could have someone measure the flour and another crack the eggs, and everyone can have a turn at stirring the dough or batter. For example, rolled, cut-out, or drop cookies are preferred over sheet cookies.

GUIDELINES FOR ADAPTATION:

During cooking time it is often natural to discuss things related to food, favorite recipes, memories of kitchen smells, helping in the kitchen, meal time rituals, etc.

It may be desirable to make some cooking projects a task for only women. A discussion could then follow concerning sex roles and how these have or have not changed.

NOTES:

COUPLETS

THERAPEUTIC VALUE:

GROUP SIZE: Small groups in competition
TIME INVOLVED: 15-45 minutes
MATERIALS NEEDED: List of well-known matching words (see list on
following page)
DESCRIPTION/DIRECTIONS: Players divide into small groups and are given a
list of words for which they are required to come up with a common match.
Groups can compete to finish their lists. Giving different lists to each group
may help avoid the problem of other groups overhearing answers.
GUIDELINES FOR ADAPTATION:
   Lower functioning individuals may benefit from having the words and
their matches printed on separate cards. The task then would be to match the
appropriate words.

   This could also be played as a *large group* activity by listing one of the
words to be matched on the chalkboard and as a group generating its pair.

   Higher functioning individuals may be asked to generate lists on their
own either alone, in pairs, or in small groups.
   Please note that there may be more than one common match beyond
those listed. Give credit for all responses that make sense.

NOTES:

COUPLET LIST

Black and White (Blue)
Odd and Even −
Adam and Eve −
Soap and Water
Bacon and Eggs −
Bread and Butter −
Coat and Tie (Hat)
Mutt and Jeff
Lock and Key −
Cap and Gown
Amos and Andy
Pen and Ink (Pencil) −
Pencil and Paper
Good and Evil (Bad) −
Bow and Arrow −
Hit and Run −
Day and Night −
Sun and Moon −
David and Goliath −

Up and Down −
Jack and Jill −
Hide and Seek −
Cats and Dogs
Meat and Potatoes
Horse and Buggy
Salt and Pepper −
Ice cream and Cake (Cookies)
Thunder and Lightning −
Cheese and Crackers
Knife and Fork (Spoon) −
Brush and Comb −
Light and Dark −
Cup and Saucer −
Romeo and Juliet −
Cream and Sugar
In and Out −
Milk and Cookies
Samson and Delilah −

CRAZY MIXED-UP STORIES

THERAPEUTIC VALUE:

GROUP SIZE: Any size

TIME INVOLVED: 10-50 minutes

MATERIALS NEEDED: Cards each with a different noun on it (e.g., baseball, snow, dog, ice cream, automobile, lamp, church, sweater, pizza, etc.)

DESCRIPTION/DIRECTIONS: The object of this task is to make up a mixed-up story using a variety of new pieces of information. The group sits in a circle and one person is selected to begin. S/he must pick a card from the stack of noun cards and use that noun to begin a short story. When s/he is finished-several sentences will do-the next person draws a card and must continue the story including the new noun in the story.

GUIDELINES FOR ADAPTATION:

Lower functioning individuals may find it too difficult to add to the previous story. They should be allowed to tell their own story. It may not be necessary to give them a card but just ask them to tell a short, crazy, and mixed-up story.

For a group of very *high functioning* individuals, both verb and noun cards can be made and used. The individual would be required to draw both a noun and a verb and to make up a story using both.

NOTES:

CURRENT EVENTS

THERAPEUTIC VALUE:

GROUP SIZE: any size

TIME INVOLVED: 15-60 minutes

MATERIALS NEEDED: Current day's newspaper

DESCRIPTION/DIRECTIONS: Participants sit in a large circle along with one or more leaders, each of whom have one or more sections of the daily newspaper. The leaders go through the paper and select major stories or stories of interest. These are summarized or read in full to the group. Participants are encouraged to react to the articles by sharing their opinions, ideas, values, and feelings.

GUIDELINES FOR ADAPTATION:

This is an activity that can be used every day and can become a regular part of a program.

Higher functioning individuals can generate lively discussions and utilize the opportunity for reminiscence. They may also enjoy sharing in the reading of selected articles to the group.

Lower functioning individuals may have a more difficult time in concentrating and may benefit more from summaries of articles rather than having a full article read. They may need more encouragement and structure in the discussion after an article is presented.

It is fun to look at the weather map of the United States and tell the temperature of the city where each group member was born (*USA TODAY* newspaper has a color weather map that works great!)

NOTES:

DEEP MUSCLE RELAXATION

THERAPEUTIC VALUE:

GROUP SIZE: Any size

TIME INVOLVED: 20-30 minutes

MATERIALS NEEDED: none

DESCRIPTION/DIRECTIONS: This is an excellent activity to reduce stress and anxiety for both the clients and the staff! Participants sit in a circle so that the leader can be seen by all and is the center of attention (modeling is important here). The leader instructs the participants to: 1) tighten a muscle and hold it; 2) notice how it feels to have that muscle tense; 3) relax that muscle; and 4) notice how it feels to relax it. Systematically tense and relax each muscle two times, beginning with the shins and proceeding to the calves, thighs, buttocks, back, stomach, forearms (clench fists), upper arms, shoulders, neck (put hand on forehead and push back keeping head straight), and face muscles. As each muscle is relaxed, encourage participants to pay attention to the tension that seems to flow out from the muscle.

GUIDELINES FOR ADAPTATION:

Dimming the lights in the room will help the participants to relax more easily. Be careful not to make the room too dark, *lower functioning* individuals need to be able to see and follow the leader's modeling.

NOTES:

DESCRIPTIONS

THERAPEUTIC VALUE:

GROUP SIZE: Any size

TIME INVOLVED: 15-60 minutes

MATERIALS NEEDED: Historical information on each of the group members

DESCRIPTION/DIRECTIONS: The group leader chooses a member to describe, without telling the group their identity. The leader then tells the group certain biographical information about this individual and the group attempts to figure out who the mystery person might be. Sketchy information should be given first (i.e., birth place; number of siblings; parents names, etc.) then more telling information could be revealed (i.e., their sex; national origin; color of hair and eyes; whether married, widowed, or divorced, etc.)

GUIDELINES FOR ADAPTATION:

   For some groups this task may be too complex. The staff may assist in the identifying process, helping *lower functioning* persons to recall the data and make some guesses. Writing the information on the chalkboard as it is presented will be helpful.

NOTES:

DILEMMA DRAMA

THERAPEUTIC VALUE:

GROUP SIZE: Any Size
TIME INVOLVED: 15-60 minutes
MATERIALS NEEDED: Ideas about dilemma dramas (see below)
DESCRIPTION/DIRECTIONS: Present a dilemma drama (i.e., a situation) to the group, which usually involves interpersonal discomfort. Ask for volunteers to play out the situation showing what they think they might do if placed in a similar circumstance.
This is a fun and creative activity that allows some participants to express themselves and others to watch the action. It can be quite entertaining.
GUIDELINES FOR ADAPTATION:
    This activity provides an opportunity to discuss and role play assertion skills.

Possible Dilemma Dramas: (needs elaboration)
1) You borrow a camera from a friend and accidently break it.
2) You're at a boring party and you want to leave but don't want to disappoint the host/hostess.
3) You're going out with a friend who is often late and you want to make sure they arrive on time so you won't be late.
4) You meet someone you've been introduced to before but now forget their name.
5) You are stuck at a party talking to someone for a long time and you want to move on to meet other people.
6) A friend sends you a gift for your birthday that you don't like but you don't want to hurt their feelings.
7) You're at a department store and you notice someone shoplifting something minor.
8) You're invited to dinner with a friend and they serve a food that you don't like to eat as a main course.

NOTES:

DRAWING FEELINGS

THERAPEUTIC VALUE:

GROUP SIZE: Any size
TIME INVOLVED: 15-30 minutes
MATERIALS NEEDED: Paper, colored pens, and pencils
DESCRIPTION/DIRECTIONS: Give each person several pieces of paper and choice of writing and drawing instruments. The leader names an emotion and each group member is to draw that feeling in whatever way they desire. Do the same with several feelings. Each person's work can be shared with the group and discussed. Others can try to guess which drawing represents which feeling.
GUIDELINES FOR ADAPTATION:
    Lower functioning individuals may not be able to follow directions well, but they may find the exercise quite enjoyable to watch.

NOTES:

EARS FOR MUSICAL ERAS

THERAPEUTIC VALUE:

GROUP SIZE: Small groups in competition
TIME INVOLVED: 15-45 minutes
MATERIALS NEEDED: Tape player, pre-recorded tape with songs from a variety of musical categories/eras.
DESCRIPTION/DIRECTIONS: Record songs from several different musical categories or eras (e.g., jazz, big band, blues, classical, rock-and-roll, chamber, folk, patriotic songs, spirituals, hymns, military songs, etc.) Play the songs and have the groups try to guess the song and/or the era. Hold a discussion about the distinguishing features of the music. Ask for examples of similar songs.
GUIDELINES FOR ADAPTATION:
    To make this activity easier, put a list of the musical categories or song names on the chalkboard or on a large piece of paper so that group members can see the options. They can then pick from the list rather than generating their own categories or titles.
    Lower functioning individuals may not be able to name the songs or categories/eras. They can be put in a group by themselves so that they can dance or move to the music without disturbing the rest of the group.
    Some songs may be familiar and everyone can sing along.

NOTES:

EXPRESSING THANKFULNESS

THERAPEUTIC VALUE:

GROUP SIZE: Any size

TIME INVOLVED: 5-30 minutes

MATERIALS NEEDED: Chalkboard

DESCRIPTION/DIRECTIONS: Focusing on the positive can be a helpful exercise. This activity helps individuals explore and express what they have to be thankful for. Write vertically on the chalkboard a word that represents a holiday or time of the year (i.e., the month or season). Using each letter in that word, have the group come up with something they are thankful for that begins with that letter. Be sure to note each person's expression of thankfulness even if it does not begin with the specified letter.

GUIDELINES FOR ADAPTATION:

   If time permits, this activity could be played using all the letters of the alphabet rather than a particular word.

NOTES:

FAIRY TALES

THERAPEUTIC VALUE:

GROUP SIZE: Any size

TIME INVOLVED: 10-60 minutes

MATERIALS NEEDED: Book of fairy tales

DESCRIPTION/DIRECTIONS: Read a fairy tale and discuss what moral or lesson is implied in the story. (e.g., Why do we teach our children these messages, Many tales are gruesome and violent, is it right to tell our children such frightening stories?) Ask about the stories they remember hearing as children.

GUIDELINES FOR ADAPTATION:

Higher functioning persons may be willing to read the stories out loud to the group. Make sure they can read loud enough, or have a microphone and amplifier available.

Lower functioning individuals may not be able to discuss the meanings of the stories but may enjoy just listening to the stories being read.

NOTES:

FAMOUS QUOTES

THERAPEUTIC VALUE:

GROUP SIZE: Any size

TIME INVOLVED: 5-45 minutes

MATERIALS NEEDED: Book of famous quotes

DESCRIPTION/DIRECTIONS: Read a quote to the group. Have the group try to guess the who, what, where, when, and why as these relate to the quote. Discuss the quote in terms of its meaning and importance. Ask the group members if they agree with the quote. Discuss additional feelings and thoughts that are stirred by the quote.

GUIDELINES FOR ADAPTATION:

Higher functioning individuals could be asked to share an example of a time when this quote may have applied to a particular life situation.

Because this is a discussion activity, it may not be appropriate for *lower functioning* individuals.

NOTES:

FEEL AND DESCRIBE

THERAPEUTIC VALUE:

GROUP SIZE: Any size

TIME INVOLVED: 15-45 minutes

MATERIALS NEEDED: 10-15 objects commonly found around the house (i.e., cotton balls, sandpaper, ping-pong ball, rubber band, etc.)

DESCRIPTION/DIRECTIONS: Objects are placed one at a time in a pillow case. This bag is passed around the group and each member feels the object in the pillow case and attempts to guess what it might be. Members may be asked to refrain from naming the object, giving descriptions of it instead. Descriptions of the object may be listed on a chalkboard as they are suggested by the group members. These can be used as clues to help figure out what the object might be.

Once it is guessed a new object is placed in the bag and the game continues.

GUIDELINES FOR ADAPTATION:

For *higher functioning* individuals a game of "See and Describe" may be played in a similar manner. In this case objects are seen by only one group member and described by him or her according to shape, color, taste, odor, size, weight, texture and function. Other members then attempt to guess what the object might be. The group leader could also be responsible for describing while the members attempt to guess.

NOTES:

FIND THE OBJECT

THERAPEUTIC VALUE:

GROUP SIZE: Any size

TIME INVOLVED: 10-40 minutes

MATERIALS NEEDED: Large paper bag, five to ten different objects

DESCRIPTION/DIRECTIONS: Place five to ten different objects into a brown paper bag. Each group member will be asked, one at a time, to reach into the bag and pull out a designated object. After they have done so, talk about how they made their decision. Was it based on shape, texture, size? Obviously some objects will be easier to distinguish from others. The easier objects can be assigned to the less impaired individuals and those with higher functioning tactile perception could be asked to make finer discriminations. Sharp and dangerous objects are obviously inappropriate.

GUIDELINES FOR ADAPTATION:

A variation on this activity would be to ask individuals to pull out the softest object, the roundest object, the hardest object, the smoothest object, etc. All objects in the bag could then be examined and compared to the one chosen.

Lower functioning individuals, too impaired to understand the directions, can be asked to pull out an object they think feels good or that they would find interesting to look at, to hold, etc.

Examples of objects: tennis ball, ping-pong ball, cotton, feather, penny, ball of string, button, steelwool, sandpaper, envelope, paper cup, wooden spoon, etc.

NOTES:

FLAGS OF THE NATIONS

THERAPEUTIC VALUE:

GROUP SIZE: Any size

TIME INVOLVED: 10-60 minutes

MATERIALS NEEDED: Book showing the flags of the different nations or actual posters of the flags (ask about these at the library), poster board or chalkboard

DESCRIPTION/DIRECTIONS: Draw a replica of a flag from a particular nation (if posters of the flags are available display it). These can be drawn on the chalkboard if different colored chalk is available, otherwise posters will need to be drawn ahead of time. After being displayed, have the group try to identify the nation from which the flag is from. Talk about various aspects of the nation. Ask who may have visited this country and ask about their impressions of this nation.

GUIDELINES FOR ADAPTATION:

To make this an easier task, display several flags along with several names of nations. Match up the nation with the name.

NOTES:

FOOD SAMPLING

THERAPEUTIC VALUE:

GROUP SIZE: Any size

TIME INVOLVED: 20-60 minutes

MATERIALS NEEDED: Food items

DESCRIPTION/DIRECTIONS: Bring in several types of food items that can be compared by taste, shape, texture, etc. (e.g., unusual fruits like papaya, mango, and kiwi, or various types of melons). Pass around the item (if possible) and have the group try to identify what it is. Encourage everyone to smell as well as feel the item. After examining the external part of the food item, cut it open or prepare it for consumption. Allow everyone to taste it if they desire. Discuss its taste and texture and compare it to other foods.

GUIDELINES FOR ADAPTATION:

This can be a very enjoyable activity for groups with all levels of impairment. *Lower functioning* individuals may enjoy just tasting the various foods, while *higher functioning* persons may want to make comments on the different items and discuss when they have enjoyed them in the past.

NOTES:

FORTUNE COOKIES

THERAPEUTIC VALUE:

GROUP SIZE: Any size

TIME INVOLVED: 10-60 minutes

MATERIALS NEEDED: Fortune cookies for everyone

DESCRIPTION/DIRECTIONS: Have each member of the group, one at a time, pull a fortune cookie out of a bag. Allow him or her to open the cookie and read their fortune. Allow that person to explain what they think about their fortune (i.e., Do they like it?, Dislike it?, Believe it?, Has it already happened?, etc.). Discussion could follow as to the beliefs of the members regarding that particular fortune and the telling of fortunes in general.

GUIDELINES FOR ADAPTATION:

You may also make a *group project* of making up your own fortunes. If you are really ambitious you could make fortune cookies from scratch and add your own fortunes.

Horoscopes can be brought in and discussed in like manner. Descriptions of the different astrological signs may also be discussed. Some individuals may have very strong feelings about horoscopes and may even be offended by their discussion. Be sensitive to this and allow them to express their feelings about this.

NOTES:

FREEDOM BALL

THERAPEUTIC VALUE:

GROUP SIZE: Any size

TIME INVOLVED: 5-30 minutes

MATERIALS NEEDED: Large ball (18 inch)

DESCRIPTION/DIRECTIONS: The group sits in a large circle. The ball is thrown, bounced, or kicked to another person in the group. It is called freedom ball because each person is free to pass it in whatever manner he or she chooses, as long as it is safe. To insure safety it may be wise to require that the ball be kept low. This game is very simple, very entertaining and gives practice in eye-hand coordination.

GUIDELINES FOR ADAPTATION:

A form of dodge ball may be adapted by having someone, preferably a staff member, stand in the center of the group and the participants attempt to hit that person with the ball.

For *higher functioning* persons adding the requirement of naming an animal, making an animal noise, naming a car model, etc., after the ball is caught. However, this may be too complex for *lower functioning* members.

NOTES:

FRIENDSHIP SQUEEZE

THERAPEUTIC VALUE:

GROUP SIZE: Any size

TIME INVOLVED: 5 minutes

MATERIALS NEEDED: none

DESCRIPTION/DIRECTIONS: Stand in a circle and have all the members hold hands. The leader begins by squeezing the hand of the person to his right or left. The squeeze is passed from person to person until it is all the way around the circle. It can then be passed the opposite direction.

GUIDELINES FOR ADAPTATION:

Lower functioning individuals may have difficulty understanding the directions and knowing when to pass the squeeze. It may be helpful to raise your hand as you squeeze so that it is visible to everyone where the squeeze is at in the circle.

NOTES:

GERONTOCRACY

THERAPEUTIC VALUE:

GROUP SIZE: Any size

TIME INVOLVED: 30-60 minutes

MATERIALS NEEDED: Chalkboard, list of possible political positions and their qualifying characteristics (see below).

DESCRIPTION/DIRECTIONS: This activity is a variation of "Strength Awards" (pg. 90). Instead of specific strengths however, the group will discuss and decide upon who in the group fits the qualifications needed for differing political offices. Begin with a particular office or position and discuss its characteristics and duties. Ask the group to examine who in the group may best fit that role. Encourage the group to examine the strengths, qualities, personal history, and likeable characteristics of the possible candidates. Focus on the positive attributes of the individuals rather than on their current ability to perform. Nominations could be announced and, based on group consensus, a member chosen or voted into the particular office.

The names and positions can be displayed on the chalkboard or on name tags made for each person.

It is important for the leader to have at least one position available for each member of the group. This may not be as difficult as it seems. Examine the list of possible positions below and compare the qualities with the members of your group.

GUIDELINES FOR ADAPTATION:

This is a great activity for groups who are together often. Groups who have an opportunity to get to know about each other over a period of time will have more to affirm and encourage in one another.

With *lower functioning* members, the staff may need to take a more active role in providing the information regarding strengths, personal history, etc.

NOTES:

GERONTOCRACY POSITIONS

Suggested Positions:	Qualifications:
President, Vice President, Prime Minister	History in similar position (i.e., retired President or V.P. of a business., etc.) Leadership skills
Secretary of Defense, Chief of Police, Sergeant at Arms, Commander of the Navy, etc.	Military history, Leadership skills, Commanding, Controlling
Foreign Minister, Secretary to United Nations, Ambassador to France, etc.	Immigrant, Speaks a foreign language, Diplomatic
Public Relations Minister, Press Secretary	Good story teller, Friendly, Good public speaker
Treasurer, Chief Accountant	Wealthy, Accounting skills
Secretary	Good social skills, Organized, Clerical skills
King, Queen, Prince, etc.	Stately, Proper, Royal lineage, Royal name
Court Jester	Jokester, Good humor, Happy
Special Envoy	Any special quality or strength
Assistant to... (any of the above)	Helpful, Supportive, Encouraging

GEROROBICS

THERAPEUTIC VALUE:

GROUP SIZE: Any size

TIME INVOLVED: 5-15 minutes

MATERIALS NEEDED: Tape player, pre-recorded music

DESCRIPTION/DIRECTIONS: Participants sit in a circle so that they can see the leader. Explain that you are going to lead some exercises that will be done while listening to music. Coordinate the type and speed of the exercise with the tempo of the music.

GUIDELINES FOR ADAPTATION:

Choose music the group members may remember or are familiar with. You may want to encourage them to sing along with the song while they move to the music.

Lower functioning individuals may require slower music and longer repetitions of the exercise or movement to allow them time to catch on and follow along.

Be aware of clients with disabilities or heart conditions that require limited strenuous physical exertion.

Allow short breaks or rest periods between songs.

NOTES:

GROUP CROSSWORD PUZZLES

THERAPEUTIC VALUE:

GROUP SIZE: Any size

TIME INVOLVED: 15-60 minutes

MATERIALS NEEDED: Any easy crossword puzzle, or part of it, written on a chalkboard

DESCRIPTION/DIRECTIONS: The group leader reads the clues and the whole group offers solution ideas. The leader fills in the puzzles as appropriate answers are given.

GUIDELINES FOR ADAPTATION:

Higher functioning members could work on puzzles in small groups or in pairs.

Similar games like Scrabble and Anagrams can be adapted as large group activities.

NOTES:

GROUP POINTS

THERAPEUTIC VALUE:

GROUP SIZE: Small groups (4-6) of equal size
TIME INVOLVED: 15-30 minutes
MATERIALS NEEDED: Paper and pencil
DESCRIPTION/DIRECTIONS: Each group is given a piece of paper and pencil and one member (or staff) is asked to record. The leader calls out items for which the group may get points. The recorder keeps track of the total points for his/her group. Leaders may need to have significant historical information on each participant readily available.

Points given for: total number of children (and/or grandchildren)
                   total of shoe sizes
                   total of ages
                   total number of watches, earrings, necklaces, rings,
                   buttons, keys, pennies,...
                   10 points for shoe laces
                   10 points for each hearing aid
                   10 points for birthdays on an even day on the month
                   5 points for glasses
                   5 points for each picture
                   5 points for nail polish on fingernails
                   5 points for each belt
                   5 points for wearing red, green, etc.
Add any additional items that seem appropriate.

GUIDELINES FOR ADAPTATION:

Utilize the skills of the group members as much as possible. Allow those who write well to write and those who can count to do so. This activity involves giving attention to each individual and it is rewarding in that each person will likely contribute in some way to the total score.

NOTES:

GROUP SENTENCE COMPLETIONS

THERAPEUTIC VALUE:

GROUP SIZE: Any size
TIME INVOLVED: 10-45 minutes
MATERIALS NEEDED: Chalkboard
DESCRIPTION/DIRECTIONS: Write an incomplete sentence on the chalkboard and ask the group to offer suggestions as to how it would be completed. List all responses and discuss their similarities and differences. Any incomplete sentence can be used but those addressing the particular problems of the group members may prove to be more emotionally stimulating. For this reason use caution and be prepared to discuss sensitive issues if they are brought up.
GUIDELINES FOR ADAPTATION:
    This could be done in a similar manner in *small groups*.

Possible Sentences:
My father was good at...
I was the only child in my family who...
When I was a child I liked to...
Sometimes I get angry at...
What I enjoyed doing with my mother was...
My best friend...
My favorite food...
One thing I like about myself is...
I look forward to...
When I feel sad I...

NOTES:

GROUP TIME LINE

THERAPEUTIC VALUE:

GROUP SIZE: Any size
TIME INVOLVED: 15-90 minutes
MATERIALS NEEDED: Time line (see below).
DESCRIPTION/DIRECTIONS: Put up a time line on a blank wall. Have each group member tell their birth date and mark these on the time line. Additional markings can be made for wedding dates, children's birthdays, and other significant personal events. Attractive stickers can be found to mark these events on the time line (e.g., hearts for wedding dates, teddy bears for children's birthdates, etc.). Add to the time line significant historical events, including president's terms in office, well known natural disasters, famous inventions, etc.

GUIDELINES FOR ADAPTATION:
　　Time lines are a helpful way for individuals to see where they have come from and what they have lived through. They also serve as a means for recognizing that there is still life ahead of them and the opportunity to create meaningful experiences.

　　Instead of marking directly on the time line, a strip of adding machine paper can be used and placed below the time line, thus making time line banners unique for each person. Markings can go on this tape. Place the banner below the time line, beginning at the year of the individual's birth.

　　Lower functioning individuals may have difficulty remembering the dates of significant events in their life, therefore having personal histories on hand may prove beneficial.

NOTES:

MAKING A TIME LINE

Time lines can be made by taping together many blank pieces of paper and drawing lines one inch apart that are labeled with years, going as far back as the oldest person in the group. See example below. Computers may also be used to generate excellent time lines.

TIME LINE

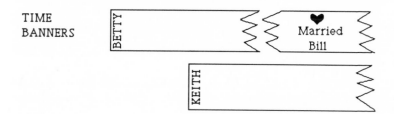

GUIDED IMAGERY

THERAPEUTIC VALUE:

GROUP SIZE: Any size
TIME INVOLVED: 20-40 minutes
MATERIALS NEEDED: none
DESCRIPTION/DIRECTIONS: Have the participants sit or lay down in a comfortable position. Ask them to close their eyes. Lead them on an internal journey using descriptors that tap all five senses. Speak slowly and clamly. Frequently repeat the instruction to close their eyes and picture what you are describing in their minds.

Imagery trips may be taken to the beach, forest, garden, ocean, lake, mountains, bakery, farm, city, mother's closet, or attic in an old house. Fantasy experiences from nature may also be enjoyable (e.g., changing from a caterpillar into a butterfly, growing from a seed into a large tree, etc.).

GUIDELINES FOR ADAPTATION:

This is one activity that is particularly vulnerable to disruption. It is important to keep the distractions to a minimum. Signs that say "Enter Quietly" may need to be posted on the door. You may find it helpful to turn the lights down in the room to give a calming effect. This activity may be more effective if the clients who are easily distracted can be involved in an alternate activity during this time.

Additional reading on stress reduction exercises, guided imagery, and relaxation strategies may provide assistance in developing the skills necessary for leading effective imagery journeys.

NOTES:

HANGMAN

THERAPEUTIC VALUE:

GROUP SIZE: Any size
TIME INVOLVED: 5-30 minutes
MATERIALS NEEDED: Chalkboard
DESCRIPTION/DIRECTIONS: Have the group sit facing the chalkboard. The leader selects a certain word and draws the appropriate number of dashes on the board. Draw the gallows above the dashes. The group members suggest letters one at a time and the leader fills in the appropriate blanks. If a letter is guessed that is not in the mystery word the leader adds a new part to the hanging man and the incorrect letter is written on the side. Guessing continues until the word is figured out or all the parts of the man are drawn and he is considered "hung".

GUIDELINES FOR ADAPTATION:

Higher functioning individuals can be responsible for generating their own words and either filling out the puzzle themselves or assisting the group leader in doing so.

Names of group members can be used. This may help simplify the game for groups of *lower functioning*.

Lower functioning individuals can draw a letter from a deck of alphabet cards (see pg. 60).

NOTES:

HAT, GLOVE, AND WHISTLE

THERAPEUTIC VALUE:

GROUP SIZE: Any size

TIME INVOLVED: 10-30 minutes

MATERIALS NEEDED: Hat, large glove, and a whistle.

DESCRIPTION/DIRECTIONS: Sit in a large circle. Pass around a hat, glove and a whistle. Each person, in turn, must put the hat and glove on and then blow the whistle. He or she then takes off the hat and glove and passes all three items to the next person.

GUIDELINES FOR ADAPTATION:

This could be played as a relay game. Two teams would sit facing each other and a hat, glove and whistle would be passed down each row. This may lead to more confusion, especially among the more severely impaired.

NOTES:

HUSH AND LISTEN

THERAPEUTIC VALUE:

GROUP SIZE: Any size
TIME INVOLVED: 5-20 minutes
MATERIALS NEEDED: None
DESCRIPTION/DIRECTIONS: Instruct the group that they are all to sit very quietly and listen carefully to the noises around them for one minute. They are requested not to talk but to just attend to the sounds they may hear. After one minute begin to talk about all the sounds. It may be helpful to list the different sounds on a chalkboard and see how many things were heard altogether.
GUIDELINES FOR ADAPTATION:
A group of *higher functioning* individuals with writing ability could do this activity individually, listening and afterwards recording for themselves all the sounds noticed.

This may be a particularly difficult or frustrating task for the *hearing impaired* and the leader should be sensitive to this.

Small groups could be assembled prior to the initial quiet phase and each group could be responsible for generating their own list of sounds heard.

NOTES:

JOURNALING

THERAPEUTIC VALUE:

GROUP SIZE: Small groups (4-8)
TIME INVOLVED: 30-90 minutes
MATERIALS NEEDED: Three ring binder, paper and pens.
DESCRIPTION/DIRECTIONS:
 Journals can be made easily by having different sheets of paper gathered in a three ring binder. The different pages can consist of different topic areas (i.e., talents, children, holidays, etc.), historical periods (i.e., the depression, Roosevelt years, the 1950's, etc.) or specific ages (preschool age, teen years, the 30's, etc.). Possible topics for different journal pages are listed below. Expand these as desired to include feelings as well as facts.
GUIDELINES FOR ADAPTATION:
 If the group is comprised of varying levels of functioning individuals the topic of the journal page to be worked on that day could be discussed in a *large group* and then only those of *higher functioning* would be asked to go into a smaller group in order to work on their individual journals.
 Lower functioning individuals may need assistance in writing and this task may be far too difficult for some. Instead of writing the *very low functioning* may find it enjoyable to look through magazines for pictures that would depict what they would want to express.

Journal Page Topics:
Grandparents
Brothers and sisters
Wedding and honeymoon
Aspirations as a child
The senses -taste, smell, touch, hearing, seeing
Times I've felt - afraid, happy, sad, proud,...
Strengths and weaknesses
Typical days activities
Major achievements
Significant life events
Fashions remembered
Past employments
Influential people in one's life
NOTES:

Parents
One's Birth
Early friendships
Favorite foods
Talents
Sports enjoyed
Sports memories
Children
Old movies
Cars owned
Nicknames
Places lived
Birthdays recalled

LETTER ASSEMBLY

THERAPEUTIC VALUE:

GROUP SIZE: Small groups in competition
TIME INVOLVED: 15-45 minutes
MATERIALS NEEDED: Alphabet Cards, one set per small group (see below)
DESCRIPTION/DIRECTIONS: Each team is given a set of cards which are either spread out for all members to view or are divided among participants. The leader calls out a word and the players attempt to put the letters together that form the word, working as quickly as possible. The first team to complete the word wins.
GUIDELINES FOR ADAPTATION:

Call out words appropriate to the season or specific to the group as a whole (i.e., names of participants, items is the room, etc.).

Call out matching word pairs, omitting the second word in the pair (i.e., salt and _____, ham and ____, etc.) and allow participants to come up with its match and spell it (see list, pg. 29). The same can be done for proverbs (see list, pg. 73) and similes (see list, pg. 64), omitting the final word in the phrase.

Higher functioning individuals can compete individually or in pairs.

Making Alphabet Cards: These cards are made by printing each letter of the alphabet on a stiff piece of cardboard (index cards or the back of business cards work well), in large enough print to be read by participants. Additional vowels and common consonants cards are useful.

NOTES:

MAGAZINE SCAVENGER HUNT

THERAPEUTIC VALUE:

?☑

GROUP SIZE: Small groups in competition

TIME INVOLVED: 20-60 minutes

MATERIALS NEEDED: Magazines to be cut up and scissors

DESCRIPTION/DIRECTIONS: Make a list (10-15 items) of easy to find items in magazines. Give a list to each small group (4-6 persons) and have them work together to find in the magazines the items on their list. The first team finding all the items are the winners. (See pg. 71 for a list of magazine items in Picture Bingo game.)

GUIDELINES FOR ADAPTATION:

For *higher functioning* individuals smaller groups and/or longer lists can be used.

Some individuals may be able to cut out pictures but not be able to find them, or vice-versa. Use the skills that are available to each individual and assist in areas of difficulty.

NOTES:

MAKING GREETING CARDS

THERAPEUTIC VALUE:

GROUP SIZE: Any size

TIME INVOLVED: 30-60 minutes

MATERIALS NEEDED: Construction paper, magazines, scissors, glue, and colored pens

DESCRIPTION/DIRECTIONS: Greeting cards can be made for ill group members, members with birthdays, or for holiday wishes. Pictures can be cut from magazines and glued to construction paper that has been folded in half like a greeting card.

GUIDELINES FOR ADAPTATION:

Encourage creativity by putting out materials such as string, yarn, glitter, and small lightweight objects (e.g., paperclips, buttons, etc.) and suggesting these may be used on the cards as well.

Lower functioning individuals may need much assistance in cutting, writing and even in finding pictures. It may be helpful for them to be instructed to find a picture that they like rather than looking for one for the purpose of making a card.

NOTES:

MATCHING SIMILES

THERAPEUTIC VALUE:

GROUP SIZE: Small groups in competition
TIME INVOLVED: 20-60 minutes
MATERIALS NEEDED: Similes (see list on following page) written out, each on a sheet of paper, omitting the last word.
DESCRIPTION/DIRECTIONS: Each small group (4-6) is given a list of incomplete similes. The group works together to finish each simile with the appropriate word. Teams compete to see who can finish the task first. It may be helpful to give each group a different list so that answers are not overheard by other teams. The lists can be rotated among the groups if time permits.
GUIDELINES FOR ADAPTATION:

This can be expanded by talking about where these similes may have originated and why.

Lower functioning groups may benefit from having the similies written out on cards with the omitted last word on another card. In this case the task would be to match the pairs.

This can be done as a *large group activity* by listing all but the last word of the simile on a chalkboard and having the group as a whole try to figure out the ending.

Higher functioning groups may enjoy generating their own list of similes, seeing how many they can come up with.

Be flexible in what you accept as a correct response. These similes can have more than one response that makes sense.

NOTES:

SIMILE LIST

Blind as a bat.
Busy as a bee.
Cold as ice.
Crazy as a loon.
Dead as a doornail.
Dry as a bone.
Easy as pie.
Fit as a fiddle.
Happy as a lark.
Hot as blazes.
Mad as a hornet.
Neat as a pin.
Playful as a kitten.
Poor as a churchmouse.
Pure as a lily
Sharp as a tack.
Slow as molasses.
Smart as a whip.
Strong as an ox.
Sweet as sugar.
Tough as shoe leather.

Bright as a dollar.
Clean as a whistle.
Clear as a bell (or crystal).
Cross as a bear.
Deaf as a post.
Dumb as a door bell.
Fast as lightning.
Flat as a pancake.
Hard as a rock.
Light as a feather.
Mad as a wet hen.
Nervous as a cat's tail.
Poor as Job's turkey.
Proud as a peacock.
Quiet as a mouse.
Slippery as an eel.
Sly as a fox.
Stiff as a poker (or board).
Sure as death.
Thin as a rail.
Ugly as sin.

MOVING STORIES

THERAPEUTIC VALUE:

GROUP SIZE: Any size
TIME INVOLVED: 5-10 minutes
MATERIALS NEEDED: Stories that have motions to be imitated. They can easily be made up as demonstrated by the example below.
DESCRIPTION/DIRECTIONS: Explain to the group that you are about to read a story that has many motions to it. The group is to follow the leader (you) as the story is read and they may feel free to make up their own motions as they see fit.
GUIDELINES FOR ADAPTATION:
Standard short stories (like fairy tales and fables) may be easily adapted. Additionally, songs and nursery rhymes can be effective (e.g., Rock-a-bye-baby, etc.).

Example of a moving story
One day, very long ago, more than five (hold up five fingers) and even more than ten (hold up ten fingers) years ago, there lived a tiny little baby (rock a baby). This child lived in a big (arms raised) house in the country. As the days went by the baby (rock) grew (move from huddled to open position) into a cute (pinch cheek) little boy. The boy learned to walk (imitate with feet) very early and he soon was running (imitate with hands and feet) all over his great big (arms raised) house. The boy's mother got tired (hand to forehead) of chasing (imitate with hands and feet) the boy around the big house and was so happy (smile) when he grew big (hands up) enough to go outside and play. (Continue by making up the story as you go.)

NOTES:

NAME DESCRIPTION

THERAPEUTIC VALUE:

GROUP SIZE: Any size
TIME INVOLVED: 20-90 minutes
MATERIALS NEEDED: Chalkboard
DESCRIPTION/DIRECTIONS: Write an individual group member's name on the chalkboard vertically. Ask the group for assistance in finding adjectives that begin with each letter of the person's name that describes that person.
GUIDELINES FOR ADAPTATION:
   It may be helpful to keep an adjective word list on hand (see Strength List, pg. 91 or Feeling List pg. 23). The leader may want to suggest a word and ask the group if they would agree.
   Instead of using adjectives, items could be found and identified in the group room that begin with the appropriate letters in a person's name.

NOTES:

NATURE WALK

THERAPEUTIC VALUE:

GROUP SIZE: Any size, as long as there is an appropriate number of staff to assist.

TIME INVOLVED: 15-60 minutes

MATERIALS NEEDED: none

DESCRIPTION/DIRECTIONS: Take the group out for a walk. Of course, weather conditions and staff assistance are necessary considerations prior to attempting this activity. Talk beforehand about what you might expect to see and hear. Suggest that they pick up certain objects and bring them back to share with the rest of the group (flowers, leaves, rocks, etc.). After the walk, talk about the sights, smells, and sounds they experienced. Allow each of the members to share the items they brought back and to talk about their experience.

GUIDELINES FOR ADAPTATION:

It may be helpful to pair up the group members and suggest that they hold hands. Having a staff member in the front and in the rear of the group is essential for safety and to keep the activity moving along.

NOTES:

ORIGIN OF A NAME

THERAPEUTIC VALUE:

GROUP SIZE: Any size

TIME INVOLVED: 20-60 minutes

MATERIALS NEEDED: A book describing the origin and meaning of names (i.e., baby book of names), paper for name tags, pen

DESCRIPTION/DIRECTIONS: After assembling the group, begin with one member and look up the meaning and origin of their first name. Discuss whether or not the meaning seems to fit the observed character of that individual. Make up a name tag that includes their name and its meaning. Do the same for all group members.

GUIDELINES FOR ADAPTATION:

A *high functioning* group member could be designated to read the meaning of each person's name. Also, someone could be responsible for writing out the names and their meanings.

If time and interest permits, the names of children and grandchildren could be discussed.

Don't forget the staff! Having the staff participate whenever possible adds to a sense of unity and equality.

NOTES:

PERSONAL CONCERNS

THERAPEUTIC VALUE:

GROUP SIZE: Any size (although small groups work well)
TIME INVOLVED: 15-60 minutes
MATERIALS NEEDED: No materials are needed however this activity may stir up many emotions and it should therefore be led by a qualified counselor who is both empathetic and supportive.
DESCRIPTION/DIRECTIONS: Ask the group as a whole to think about what is concerning them most in their life right now. Allow some time for reflection and then ask for volunteers to share with the group their most pressing concerns. The leader should respond empathically and encourage the other group members to share their care and support. Allow as many people to share as possible, taking time to really listen to the concerns of each member.
GUIDELINES FOR ADAPTATION:
   Lower functioning groups may benefit from having several categories of concerns listed on the chalkboard from which they could pick one or several (i.e., family, health, boredom, friends, etc.). Again, encourage them to share as fully as they desire providing them a safe and caring environment.

NOTES:

PET A PET

THERAPEUTIC VALUE:

GROUP SIZE: Any size

TIME INVOLVED: 30-60 minutes

MATERIALS NEEDED: Live animals (pets) or pictures of pets

DESCRIPTION/DIRECTIONS: The staff can arrange to have one of the group members bring a pet for part of the day, or a staff member could bring in a pet (or possibly arrange with the humane society, animal protection agency, or pet store to bring in a pet). Clients can touch and hold the animals as they please, allowing them to give and receive some affection. This activity can lead into a discussion of past or present pets. Fears, joys, losses, and other emotions can be explored. Discussions on favorite pets, unusual pets, and favorite pet stories can easily follow.

GUIDELINES FOR ADAPTATION:

If bringing in pets is not feasible or recommended for your group, pictures of pets could be used in their place. Obviously, this will not allow for the same physical or emotional stimulation but it can lead to a wonderful group discussion.

NOTES:

PICTURE BINGO

THERAPEUTIC VALUE:

GROUP SIZE: Any size

TIME INVOLVED: 15-45 minutes

MATERIALS NEEDED: Picture Bingo cards and chips or markers to cover pictures. The cards can be made as a separate group activity (see below).

DESCRIPTION/DIRECTIONS: This game is played like regular Bingo except that the leader calls out the name of an object rather than a number. The objects can be listed on separate slips of paper and drawn from a hat or listed on a sheet of paper and picked at random. The participants look for a picture of that object on their Picture Bingo card and if found cover it up with a chip or marker. The first person to get a row of items covered wins. A back rub is an excellent prize for the winner.

GUIDELINES FOR ADAPTATION:

It may be useful to have participants involved in pulling the object name from the hat and reading it aloud. Make sure the individual has the appropriate visual and reading skills prior to this request.

Making Picture Bingo Cards: These cards can be a fun project to create as a group activity. Take large sheets of construction paper and divide it into uniform squares making a five by five grid, each square approximately 3x3 inches. Write the name of pictures, that can easily be found in magazines (see list below), in each of the squares. Give each person a card and several magazines and assist them in finding pictures that match the word on their card. Cut out and paste these pictures onto the card in the appropriate square. It may be easier to make this a small group project.

Suggested pictures: cat, dog, boy, girl, bird, house, tree, ice cream, cake, flowers, fruit, hat, kleenex, chair, horse, fork, spoon, recipe, coffee, plate, car,cigarette, boat, map, camera, baby, book, telephone, ring, cheese, aspirin, razor, comb, credit card, watch, beer, wine, hard liquor, cup, world, bicycle motorcycle,...

NOTES:

PROVERBS

THERAPEUTIC VALUE:

GROUP SIZE: Any size

TIME INVOLVED: 10-60 minutes

MATERIALS NEEDED: Proverbs list (see below) and chalkboard

DESCRIPTION/DIRECTIONS: Write the beginning of a proverb on the chalkboard and have the group finish it off correctly (e.g., Don't count your chickens before ...*they hatch*). Discuss the meaning of the proverb and ask for personal examples of when this proverb has applied to someone's life.

GUIDELINES FOR ADAPTATION:

This could be done as a *small group activity* by giving each small group a list of incomplete proverbs and having them work together to finish each one appropriately. They could then discuss, as a small group, the meaning of each proverb and give personal examples of it.

Small groups could also be given a proverb that has each word in the saying on a different small piece of paper. The task then would be to put the words together in the proper order to make the appropriate proverb.

Members could also be asked for their favorite proverb or one that has helped them in their life.

NOTES:

PROVERB LIST

A man is known by the company he keeps.
A penny saved is a penny earned.
A rotten apple spoils the whole barrel. --
A stitch in time saves nine. --
A watched pot never boils. --
Absence makes the heart grow fonder. --
Actions speak louder than words.
After the storm comes the calm. --
All's fair in love and war. --
All that glitters is not gold. --
April showers bring May flowers.
Beauty is only skin deep. --
Beggars cannot be choosers. --
Better late than never.   --
Birds of a feather flock together. --
Blood is thicker than water. --
Curiosity killed the cat.--
Don't count your chickens before they're hatched.--
Don't judge a book by its cover. --
Don't put off until tomorrow what you can do today.
Easy come, easy go.
Every rose has its thorn. --
Forewarned is forearmed. --
God helps those who help themselves. --
Health is better than wealth.
Honesty is the best policy. --
If at first you don't succeed, try, try again. --
It's easier said than done. --
Let sleeping dogs lie. --
Like father, like son. --
Misery loves company. --
Out of sight, out of mind.
People in glass houses shouldn't throw stones. --
Rome wasn't built in a day. --
Silence is golden.   --
Still water runs deep. --
The early bird catches the worm. --
The road to hell is paved with good intentions.--
Too many chiefs and not enough indians. --
Too many cooks spoil the broth. --
Where there's a will, there's a way. --
You can lead a horse to water, but you can't make him drink. --

PULSE GOLF

THERAPEUTIC VALUE:

GROUP SIZE: Small groups of four
TIME INVOLVED: 10-30 minutes
MATERIALS NEEDED: Watch or clock with second hand, chalkboard
DESCRIPTION/DIRECTIONS: This is an activity similar to "Group Points" in that everybody, regardless of impairment, can feel like they are participating and contributing to their team.
Divide all the members into teams of four, just like in regular golf. Explain to the group that each person's pulse will be taken and the beats per minute will be recorded as that person's "golf score." A one minute pulse is quite close to a reasonable score in 18-hole golf (approx. 65 - 120). Record each score on the "leader board" (chalkboard). Award a prize to the team with the lowest combined score and to the lowest individual score.
GUIDELINES FOR ADAPTATION:
This activity can be done on a regular basis to monitor the health of group members or to examine the results of an exercise program.
Higher functioning individuals may enjoy participating in a discussion of health issues. Nutrition, exercise, and mental health issues may provide an interesting discussion.
Those who previously or currently play golf may find this activity a jumping off point for sharing about their golf experiences. They may want to compare their pulse score with previous golf scores.

NOTES:

RECALL

THERAPEUTIC VALUE:

GROUP SIZE: Small group (4-8)
TIME INVOLVED: 15-60 minutes
MATERIALS NEEDED: 30 small objects that can easily be identified and a tray.
DESCRIPTION/DIRECTIONS: Place 10 objects on a tray and allow the group to look at the objects for only several minutes. Take the objects away and see how many can be recalled as a group. Place ten different objects on the tray but this time allow the objects to be passed around the group so each person has a chance to feel each one. Again take away the objects and attempt to recall what was seen. Finally, take the last 10 items and discuss each one, making an association of each object with some aspect of the group. Remove the items again and test for recall.

This provides an opportunity for discussing memory and noticed changes in memory ability. Talk about the ways in which the three methods of examining the items differed and which seemed more helpful. Discuss ways in which we can help ourselves to remember things, such as keeping notes.
GUIDELINES FOR ADAPTATION:

This may be an activity in which small groups could compete to see which group could generate the longest list of recalled items.

This task may be frustrating for individuals who are aware of *memory impairment*. This frustration may be lessened by not asking them directly to recall items. The task can provide them an opportunity to discuss their frustration with their present condition.

NOTES:

REMEMBER WHEN...

THERAPEUTIC VALUE:

GROUP SIZE: Any size
TIME INVOLVED: 15-60 minutes
MATERIALS NEEDED: None
DESCRIPTION/DIRECTIONS: There are many topics to discuss with older adults that reflect the changes in our society over the past century. Older persons enjoy sharing about life as they remember it. Several topic areas are listed below but the actual number of topics are endless.

Ask questions like, "How are things different today?" "What things are still the same?" "What changes have you seen in this area in your life time?" "What do you miss about the good old days?"

GUIDELINES FOR ADAPTATION:

Personal reflections from the past can also be topics of group discussions. (See Journaling, page 59 for suggested topics)

Memorabilia of the different topic areas can also be brought in, if available, to stimulate the discussion.

Suggested Topic areas:
Fashions - hair, clothing, shoes
Transportation - planes, cars, boats, space travel
Communication systems - telephone, television, radio
Education - schools, discipline, value of education
Entertainment - movies, sports
Recreation - toys, vacations
Wars
Politics
Household conveniences - washers, dryers, dishwashers, stoves, refrigerators
Currency - coin designs, what you used to get for a nickel
Child rearing methods
Religion

NOTES:

RHYMING WORDS

THERAPEUTIC VALUE:

GROUP SIZE: Any size

TIME INVOLVED: 5-30 minutes

MATERIALS NEEDED: none

DESCRIPTION/DIRECTIONS: This is a simple yet fun and creative activity. The leader of the group suggests a word, or asks any participant for a word, and the group combines its efforts to generate as many possible rhymes to the word suggested. These words can be listed on a chalkboard or just acknowledged as they are offered.

GUIDELINES FOR ADAPTATION:

This may also be played as a *small group* competition game, similar to Couplets (pg. 28). Groups could compete in generating the longest list of possible rhymes to one or more words.

Four letter words like sing, long, bell, tack, etc., have many rhyming words and seem to work best for this activity.

NOTES:

RHYTHM ECHO

THERAPEUTIC VALUE:

GROUP SIZE: Any size
TIME INVOLVED: 5-15 minutes
MATERIALS NEEDED: none
DESCRIPTION/DIRECTIONS: The leader makes up simple rhythms by snapping his or her fingers, and/or slapping hands or legs. Group members attempt to imitate this rhythm. Begin with easy rhythms and progressively get more complex. Rhythms can also be sped up.
GUIDELINES FOR ADAPTATION:
     For *higher functioning* group members, allow them to make up rhythms that the group can copy.

NOTES:

ROLL-A-QUESTION

THERAPEUTIC VALUE:

GROUP SIZE: Any size

TIME INVOLVED: 10-45 minutes

MATERIALS NEEDED: Dice and cards with simple questions, written in large print. (Cards can include questions about favorite activities, foods, colors, ice cream, beverages, vacations, animals, seasons, etc.. Questions can also be asked about feelings, thoughts, memories, beliefs, relationships, etc..)

DESCRIPTION/DIRECTIONS: The participants sit in a large circle. One person begins by rolling the dice. The number on the dice indicates the number of seats to the right of the person rolling the dice. The individual in this seat must choose a question card from the stack of cards and must answer the question before rolling the dice and having the next person draw a card. The leader of this activity may need to read the question and help the individual to answer.

GUIDELINES FOR ADAPTATION:

Incomplete sentences may be used instead of questions (e.g., I was happiest when I ...). See pg. 52 for a list of sentences.

One large die that can be rolled on the floor and seen by everyone works best.

NOTES:

SCRAMBLED WORDS

THERAPEUTIC VALUE:

GROUP SIZE: Small groups in competition
TIME INVOLVED: 5-30 minutes
MATERIALS NEEDED: Several sets of Alphabet cards (see pg. 60)
DESCRIPTION/DIRECTIONS: Break into small groups of 4 to 6 persons. Give each group specific letters of the alphabet that, when unscrambled, will spell a commonly known word. Teams compete for the fastest solution to the scrambled words.
GUIDELINES FOR ADAPTATION:
    Each team may be given different scrambled words of the same length.
    Once the word is unscrambled the teams could go on to see how many other words they could make out of the letters that were used to form the initial word. Teams could compete for the longest list.

    This activity could also be done as a *large group activity* where the scrambled word is written on a chalkboard and the group as a whole attempts to unscramble it.

NOTES:

SELF COLLAGES

THERAPEUTIC VALUE:

GROUP SIZE: Any size

TIME INVOLVED: 30-60 minutes

MATERIALS NEEDED: Magazines, scissors, paste, and construction paper

DESCRIPTION/DIRECTIONS: Give the participants the following instructions, "We are going to create collages depicting different aspects of ourselves. I want you to look through the magazines and find pictures of things that represent your "real self", that is, the part of you that is visible for others to see. Also I want you to find pictures that represent your "hidden self", that is, the part of you that is more hidden, maybe your wishes, dreams or secrets." Allow the members to leisurely explore magazines and cut out these pictures. Posters can be made of pictures depicting their "real self" and their "hidden self". These can be shared with the group and discussed.

GUIDELINES FOR ADAPTATION:

The more impaired individuals may have difficulty with understanding the project. The instructions could be modified, telling them to look for pictures they find appealing, or to look for anything they like. The staff and other group members may help by finding pictures or words they think represent these individuals and give these to them.

NOTES:

SENSE OF SCENT

THERAPEUTIC VALUE:

GROUP SIZE: Any size

TIME INVOLVED: 15-60 minutes

MATERIALS NEEDED: Small pouches in which "smelly" items can be placed and smelled without being seen.

DESCRIPTION/DIRECTIONS: One at a time pass around the group a pouch containing an item with a *strong* scent. These may include dried onion, bacon bits, tea, coffee, cocoa, orange rind, lemon rind, cheese (if not too greasy), pepper, honeysuckle, gardenia, curry powder, cloves, extracts (small amount poured on cotton ball), or other items. As they are passed have the participants try to identify each item and/or talk about whether the scent is pleasant or not. The stronger the scent, the better.

GUIDELINES FOR ADAPTATION:

This can be *expanded* by talking about the scents in more detail, such as memories and experiences related to that particular smell and exploring smells that are similar.

For the *higher functioning* persons this could be played as a guessing game in which the items were passed and each participant would record their guess as to the contents of the pouch. Responses could then be compared.

Instead of bringing in the real item to smell, the popular Scratch and Sniff stickers could be used. These are stickers that, when the surface is scratched, produce odors of flowers, bubble gum, root beer, etc.. They are available in stationery and party stores. (These stickers make excellent prizes for games as well.)

NOTES:

SHARING CARING

THERAPEUTIC VALUE:

GROUP SIZE: Any size
TIME INVOLVED: 15-40 minutes
MATERIALS NEEDED: Care sharing list (see next page) and chalkboard
DESCRIPTION/DIRECTIONS: Use the care sharing list to discuss the various ways in which care and concern are expressed. Explore the ways individuals in the group feel about the different methods of expression. Discuss how each person would like to give and receive expressions of caring. The leader may share ways s/he has observed the group sharing affection.
GUIDELINES FOR ADAPTATION:
     After the discussion the members may choose to express their caring of other group members in ways that are comfortable for them.

NOTES:

CARE SHARING LIST

Verbal Expressions

Directly sharing feelings: "I really like you."
Indirectly sharing feelings: "I really liked our time together today."
Compliments about appearance: "You look pretty."
Compliments about actions: "I liked the way you helped him."
Appreciation of personal characteristics and traits: "You're a very gentle person."
Using an affectionate name: "Hey cutie"

Non-Verbal Expressions

A smile
A wink
A kiss
A hug
Holding hands
A pat on the shoulder or back
A neck or back rub

Other Expressions

Listening and giving understanding
Sharing personal feelings, thoughts, dreams
Offering a helping hand
Choosing to sit by someone
Dancing together
Giving gifts

SIMILARITIES AND DIFFERENCES

THERAPEUTIC VALUE:

?

GROUP SIZE: Small groups in competition (adapt for large group)
TIME INVOLVED: 20-60 minutes
MATERIALS NEEDED: Pairs of items that have similarities (i.e., straight pin
and safety pin, pen and pencil, bowl and a pan, fork and spoon,...)
DESCRIPTION/DIRECTIONS: Give each small group a pair of items. Ask them
to list how these items are similar and how they are different. A staff
member may be needed to list the items and to help in generating the lists.
Switch the items between the groups and make new lists. When all the
groups have seen and listed the similarities and differences of all of the items
compare the responses and discuss.

GUIDELINES FOR ADAPTATION:
More complex pairs of items can be used to generate more creative lists of
differences and similarities.
This can be done as a *large group* activity. The leader would hold up or
pass around two items and the group as a whole would list how the items
were similar and different. Responses could be listed on a chalkboard.

NOTES:

SLIDE SHOWS

THERAPEUTIC VALUE:

GROUP SIZE: Any size

TIME INVOLVED: 20-60 minutes

MATERIALS NEEDED: Slide projector, slides of famous art (or various scenes)

DESCRIPTION/DIRECTIONS: Slides of famous art are often available to be checked out from libraries. Present these slides to the group. As each slide is shown, have the group members guess the artist, name of the painting, time period, or share their opinions, ideas, values, and feelings that are elicited by the piece of art.

GUIDELINES FOR ADAPTATION:

If works of art are not available to you, try substituting slides of various scenes (e.g., countryside, urban areas, mountains, deserts, people, or whatever). Choose pictures that may elicit strong feelings, opinions or ideas.

Using slides (or a video) taken of the individual group members often produces an interesting discussion.

NOTES:

SOUND IDENTIFICATION

THERAPEUTIC VALUE:

GROUP SIZE: Any size
TIME INVOLVED: 10-30 minutes
MATERIALS NEEDED: Tape recorder, tape of recorded sounds.
DESCRIPTION/DIRECTIONS: Play recorded sounds of commonly heard things (i.e., garbage disposal, birds, children, toilet flushing, kettle boiling, clock ticking, clock striking, electric mixer, toaster popping, waves crashing, door creaking, etc.). One at a time allow the group to identify the sounds and talk about them.
GUIDELINES FOR ADAPTATION:
For *hearing impaired* individuals this task may be difficult. Putting a microphone next to the tape player will help amplify the sound.

A recording of each of the group members voices can also be made. These can be played back and individuals may guess as to whose voice they are hearing.

NOTES:

SOOTHING HANDS

THERAPEUTIC VALUE:

GROUP SIZE: Pairs

TIME INVOLVED: 5-10 minutes

MATERIALS NEEDED: Hand cream

DESCRIPTION/DIRECTIONS: Pair up all the group members and have them sit facing their partner, close enough to hold hands. Put hand cream on one of the individuals hands and instruct them to rub it into their partners hands. When they are finished, switch and have their partner do the same.

GUIDELINES FOR ADAPTATION:

This is excellent for older persons whose hands are often dry and in need of the moisture. It is also a safe way of touching and expressing caring nonverbally.

This could lead into discussions on how it feels to be touched, memories of others touching us, etc.

NOTES:

SPOTLIGHTING

THERAPEUTIC VALUE:

GROUP SIZE: Any size
TIME INVOLVED: 10-90 minutes
MATERIALS NEEDED: none
DESCRIPTION/DIRECTIONS: Participants sit in a circle. The leader chooses someone or asks for a volunteer and this person is interviewed by the other group members. Any member may ask a question, which may be declined by the interviewee if he or she chooses.

Questions may include asking about favorite colors, foods, ice cream, beverages, vacation spots, animals, vegetables, seasons. Historical information may be of interest (i.e., marriages, children, birthplace, places lived, etc.)

GUIDELINES FOR ADAPTATION:

For *lower functioning* individuals it may be necessary to have pertinent historical information available on the individual being spotlighted.

It may be useful to use a chalkboard to write up the information obtained on each individual as they are spotlighted. This could then be reviewed at the end of the interview.

Members of the group could be asked what they have learned about the individual spotlighted that they did not know about them before.

NOTES:

STRENGTH AWARDS

THERAPEUTIC VALUE:

GROUP SIZE: Any size

TIME INVOLVED: 30-60 minutes (larger groups need more time)

MATERIALS NEEDED: Award ribbons (see diagram below), strength list (see next page)

DESCRIPTION/DIRECTIONS: List a variety of strengths (see list next page) on a chalkboard or poster and briefly discuss the meaning of each. As a group, discuss the particular strengths of each individual in turn and designate a particular strength that the group agrees is suitable for that person. Write this strength, in bold letters, on the ribbon and pin it on each participant.

GUIDELINES FOR ADAPTATION:

Allow the group to discuss freely the strengths seen in each other. In some cases the staff may need to assist in coming up with positive qualities for difficult individuals. This can be a very supportive and unifying activity. Each person is left feeling valuable and noticed.

The Feeling List (pg. 23) can provide additional words that can be used as strengths.

NOTES:

STRENGTH LIST

able
active
adaptable
adjusted
benevolent
brave
bright
busy
calm
capable
careful
caring
certain
charming
cheerful
clever
cooperative
courageous
creative
dedicated
dependable
determined
easy going
efficient
empathic
energetic
even tempered
exact
extroverted
faithful
forceful
foresightful
forthright
friendly
full of ideas
generous
gentle
goal setter
go-getter
good looking
growing
happy
healthy

helpful
honest
honorable
humble
humorous
imaginative
independent
industrious
initiator
instructive
intelligent
intuitive
jovial
joyful
just
kind
leader
likes new ideas
lively
looked up to
magnetic
manager
mature
musical
neat
openminded
optimistic
orderly
original
outgoing
overcoming
participator
passionate
peaceful
persevering
persistent
planner
productive
realistic
respected
searching
self-aware
self-confident

self-directed
sharp
stable
straightforward
thinker
tireless
trusting
trusted
understanding
vivacious
well-informed
wise
zealous
zestful

STRETCH YOUR IMAGINATION

THERAPEUTIC VALUE:

GROUP SIZE: Any size
TIME INVOLVED: 10-40 minutes
MATERIALS NEEDED: Imagination stretcher ideas (see below)
DESCRIPTION/DIRECTIONS: Tell the group they will be asked to stretch their imaginations and think of as many things as they can that fit the particular situation. List all the responses on the chalkboard and discuss their appropriateness.
GUIDELINES FOR ADAPTATION:
   Small groups could compete to list as many things as possible.
   Group members could be made responsible for coming up with different categories to explore.
   Lower functioning individuals or those that cannot speak may not be suitable for this activity. Dividing these individuals into small groups containing higher functioning members may be a more appropriate way to include them in this activity.`

Sample imagination stretchers:
Name things that are small enough to fit in a medicine bottle. (Bring in a bottle so they can see the size.)
Name as many things as you can that hop.
Name as many things as you can that are bigger than this room.
Name as many things as you can that can be folded in half.
Name as many white things as you can that can be poured.
Name as many things as you can that can crack.
Name as many things as you can that are meant to be hit.

NOTES:

TWENTY QUESTIONS

THERAPEUTIC VALUE:

GROUP SIZE: Any size
TIME INVOLVED: 5-30 minutes
MATERIALS NEEDED: none
DESCRIPTION/DIRECTIONS: This is an old familiar game that most of us played as children. One member of the group or staff thinks of an object, either animal, vegetable, or mineral. The other group members then may ask 20 "yes" or "no" questions to try and figure out what the object is. The staff can help to guide the questioning. The score can be kept on a chalkboard.
GUIDELINES FOR ADAPTATION: *Lower functioning* individuals with memory or concentration difficulties may need to tell the leader what the item is to prevent possible confusion.

Higher functioning individuals often take over the questioning and monopolize the activity. They may need to be gently reminded to give others a chance.

NOTES:

THROW IT

THERAPEUTIC VALUE:

GROUP SIZE: Any size

TIME INVOLVED: 5-45 minutes

MATERIALS NEEDED: Some of the following objects from each category are needed

Category A - Objects

balls -	coins
tennis, rubber, beach,	cotton ball
nerf, ping-pong	paper plates
buttons	bottle caps
balloons	feathers
paper airplanes	drinking straws
bean bags	paper cups

Category B - Containers

box	bucket
laundry basket	hat
bowl	egg cartons
muffin tins	

DESCRIPTION/DIRECTIONS: Use one or several of the objects from Category A and throw them *into* any of the objects in Category B. Have the group members compare the difference in the difficulty of throwing the items.

GUIDELINES FOR ADAPTATION:

These items can also be thrown through a hoop or to targets marked on the floor.

Contests could take place between members as to who could throw items the farthest (using objects like straws, paper plates, paper cups, balloons).

Relays could also be conducted between teams passing a specified item down the row, over their heads, or between their legs.

Teams can compete against each other by giving different point values for items in Category B and different multiplier values for items in Category A. Each team member can then choose an object and throw it into a container.

Example:

Category A	*Category B*
Bean bag =1x	Large box = 5 pts.
Rubber ball = 2x	Medium box = 10 pts.
Balloon = 10x	Small box = 20 pts.

e.g., If bean bag is thrown into medium box, then total points equals 10. If balloon is thrown into large box, then total points is 50 (5 x 10).

NOTES:

VALUE CHOICES

THERAPEUTIC VALUE:

GROUP SIZE: Any size
TIME INVOLVED: 15-60 minutes
MATERIALS NEEDED: List of values and chalkboard
DESCRIPTION/DIRECTIONS: List three values on the chalkboard and ask the group members individually to choose the one they would value most and why. Allow for as much discussion as possible, encouraging people to share openly about their values.
GUIDELINES FOR ADAPTATION:
   This activity could be done in *small groups* as well.
   This activity may be too complex for *lower functioning* individuals.

Possible Values:
To live in beautiful surroundings.
To contribute to the happiness of others.
To know everything I want to know
To love my fellowman.
To be able to do what I want to do.
To be alone whenever I want.
To be free from worry.
To have a satisfying religious life.
To have a happy family life.
To be in good health.
To have all the money I want.
To be successful.
To give and receive love.
To be famous.
To have a satisfying marriage.
To be sexually attractive.
To live in a society free from discrimination.
To be able to help others succeed
To have the opportunity to influence other people.
To have friends who understand and accept me.

NOTES:

WAD BALL

THERAPEUTIC VALUE:

GROUP SIZE: 5-15 participants
TIME INVOLVED: 20-50 minutes
MATERIALS NEEDED: Large plastic baseball bat, old newspapers or magazines
DESCRIPTION/DIRECTIONS: This is an active game that can easily get out of hand, but it is also a lot of fun. Time needs to be allowed for clean up when the game is over. One individual is chosen to be the defender. S/he sits in front of a large box or waste paper basket, holding the bat. All other participants sit in a half circle in front of the defender. They are given sheets of newspaper or magazine pages which they are instructed to wad into a ball and attempt to throw it into the box in front of the defender. The defender tries to keep as many wads of paper out of the box as possible, using the bat to hit away the paper as it is thrown.
GUIDELINES FOR ADAPTATION:

Lower functioning individuals may not be able to catch on to the rules and may throw the paper at others in the group rather than into the box. This may need to be monitored so as not to get too disruptive. However, the activity of crumpling up the paper and throwing it is good exercise and is not likely to be dangerous. A spirit of fun must accompany this activity.

NOTES:

WHO AM I?

THERAPEUTIC VALUE:

GROUP SIZE: Any size

TIME INVOLVED: 5-30 minutes

MATERIALS NEEDED: Information about famous persons

DESCRIPTION/DIRECTIONS: Explain to the group that you are thinking of someone famous. Their task is to figure out who this person is based on clues given by the leader. Weak clues are given first and are followed by stronger clues (e.g., I had wooden teeth, I was born in 1735, people say I never told a lie, I chopped down a cherry tree as a child, I was the first president of the United States - George Washington).

GUIDELINES FOR ADAPTATION:

Higher functioning individuals may be able to pick a famous individual and come up with appropriate clues.

NOTES:

WHO IS IT ?

THERAPEUTIC VALUE:

GROUP SIZE: Any size

TIME INVOLVED: 5-30 minutes

MATERIALS NEEDED: none

DESCRIPTION/DIRECTIONS: Explain to the group that you are thinking of someone in the room and their task is to ask yes or no questions to figure out who this person is. Guidance may be given to help them get key information (i.e., is it a male or female, are they wearing blue,etc.).

GUIDELINES FOR ADAPTATION:

Higher functioning individuals may be able to pick a person and answer the group's questions as they attempt to identify the individual.

NOTES:

WHOSE FACE IS IT ?

THERAPEUTIC VALUE:

GROUP SIZE: Any size (adapt to small group competition)
TIME INVOLVED: 5-45 minutes
MATERIALS NEEDED: Pictures of well known persons, the larger the better.
DESCRIPTION/DIRECTIONS: A picture of a well known person is shown to the group. Members try to guess the name of the person. Discussion could follow about the individual and their popularity.
GUIDELINES FOR ADAPTATION:

In *small groups* the members could compete with each other to see who could come up with the most names in the shortest amount of time. Different sets of pictures could be used or the same set could be rotated between the groups.

For *lower functioning* individuals the names of the well known persons could also be given and the task would be one of matching the name with the picture.

If the famous face is not guessed right away, descriptive clues could be given (i.e., tell why the person is famous, when s/he lived, etc.).

NOTES:

WISDOM OF THE AGES POSTERS

THERAPEUTIC VALUE:

GROUP SIZE: Any size

TIME INVOLVED: Several minutes each day over several months time

MATERIALS NEEDED: Poster board, colored pens

DESCRIPTION/DIRECTIONS: Like most of us many impaired older adults will have a favorite saying, poem, story, proverb, motto, or song that they have shared or could share with the group. The group leaders can encourage the sharing of such things and keep accounts of them. These can be collected and displayed in the group room in some attractive fashion. They could be calligraphied or nicely printed on poster board. One poster can be made for each individual with comments about why he or she liked that particular selection.

GUIDELINES FOR ADAPTATION:

A collage poster can be made as a *large group activity*. Each individual can pick a small proverb or line from a song and these could be collected and all placed on the same poster. This activity could lead to a marvelous group discussion about people's beliefs, motivations and feelings.

NOTES:

WORLD RECORDS

THERAPEUTIC VALUE:

GROUP SIZE: Any size
TIME INVOLVED: 10-30 minutes
MATERIALS NEEDED: Book of world records (e.g., *Guiness Book of World Records*)
DESCRIPTION/DIRECTIONS: Read about particular world records and allow the group members to discuss them. Leave room for the participants to guess about particular records (i.e., What was the weight of the heaviest man to ever live? How long were the longest fingernails? What was the fastest mile ever run? etc.).
GUIDELINES FOR ADAPTATION:

For *lower functioning* individuals it would be appropriate to ask "yes" or "no" and "true" or "false" questions. They could also answer some questions non-verbally (e.g., show us how long you think the longest fingernails were).

A prize or award could be given to the person who makes the closest guess to the actual world record.

NOTES:

WORKING WITH CRAFTS

There are many different craft ideas that can be used successfully with impaired older adults. Proper supervision is needed and special attention should be given for the more highly impaired individuals. Children's books of crafts may be a helpful resource. Listed below are some of the crafts that we have used. This list is far from complete but it will give you ideas about how crafts can be used and modified when working with this population.

Cutting Snowflakes - is a favorite Christmas craft. Paper is folded in half again and again and then small cuts are made with scissors and the sections are removed. The paper is then unfolded and the cut out designs resemble the shape of a snowflake.

Paper chains - is another Christmas craft. Colored paper is cut into strips of equal size (1" x 6" works well). Beginning with one strip, loop it and staple. The next piece is looped through the first and stapled, and so on. Chains can then be strung around the room as decorations.

Collages - can be made of various topics: Pictures of men, women, older persons, children, food groups, wishes, expressions of different feelings, etc. These can be made into attractive posters to be placed in the group room.

Musical Instruments - can be made simply and inexpensively. Paper plates stapled together after dried beans, peas, or macaroni have been placed inside make excellent rhythm instruments. Old plastic containers with lids that can be glued on are also effective. The outside of the instruments may be colored or decorated with yarn. These instruments can be brought out during singing time, although too many instruments of this type will be noisy. You may think of other creative ways to make different musical instruments.

Fingerpainting - can be fun but messy. Sleeves need to be rolled up and aprons put on if available. Use pudding as the fingerpaint. It is not dangerous if eaten and dries like fingerpaint would. Handprints can be made on separate paper.

Clay - is also a common craft item. Harmless clay can be made of salt and flour (see craft books for recipes) and this hardens and can eventually be painted. Have items available to utilize with the clay (i.e., popsicle sticks, coins or other objects that leave an imprint, etc.)

Stringing Macaroni - with yarn (the larger sizes are better). The macaroni can be painted before or after stringing. Once strung, they can be used as room decorations or jewelry.

Potato Stamps - are made by cutting potatoes into different shapes and using them as stamps to make different prints. Lower functioning individuals may not be capable of cutting the potatoes without hurting themselves. They may still enjoy making prints. Stamp pads can be used to make the prints.

Pipecleaner Art - involves cutting and twisting different pipecleaners together to form various shapes. They can be found in different colors.

Stringing Popcorn - is a favorite Christmas time activity. It is not recommended for those without the fine motor coordination necessary to avoid pricking themselves. A somewhat dull needle will work fine.

Masks from Paper Bags - this is a fun one at Halloween. Take a large brown paper bag and draw a face on. Cut out the eyes and mouth. Yarn can be glued on for hair. Color with crayons or felt pens.

Valentines - are fun on Valentine's Day. Use construction paper, doilies, and magazines for pictures.

Generating Your Own Activities

Knowing how to generate your own activities will leave you with a never ending supply of activity ideas. Here are several suggestions and ideas we would like to propose for helping you to develop your own activities.

1. **Explore your own likes and interests.** If it is interesting to you it may have some interest to others as well. Bringing in your own hobbies and sharing them can be quite entertaining.

2. **Use existing reference materials.** Be creative in looking for resources. There are plenty of good ones out there but very few in the geriatric section of the library. Check the following locations for the suggested materials:

Library:

    Game books and magazines

    Educational and musical tapes

    Movies and slide shows

    Story and poem books

    Children's craft books

Bookstores:

    Journals for grandparents (These can be modified to suit your needs)

    Tapes of old radio shows

    Colorful books on geography, history, food, people, animals, etc.

    Songbooks of old songs - in large print

School supply stores:

    Stimulating stories with discussion questions

    Room decorating ideas (seasonal and educative, see suggestions below)

    Teaching tools (e.g., history, creativity enhancement, nutrition, etc.)

3. **Use existing games.** There are many games that can be used as they are or modified slightly to suit the needs of your group. Using these games and activities in a large group setting will allow individual deficits to be overshadowed by the competency of others who do not share the same limitation. Thus, the group as a whole experiences success and every member in the group can share in this. We have listed several here:

Bean Bag Toss (Tic-Tac-Toe)

Ring Toss

Horse Shoes (rubber)

Plastic bowling ball and pins

Shuffleboard

Suction Darts

Memory Game

Mad Libs

Bingo

Checkers (regular and Chinese)

Playing cards (large cards are available)

Scrabble

Jigsaw puzzles

Parcheesi

Dominoes

4. **Use existing services.** Schools and service clubs may offer different community services of interest. Magicians, musicians, lecturers, and other entertainers may be available in your community. Make sure you describe the type of program you are leading so the guests will know what to expect. It may be advisable to keep guest visits short as the unfamiliarity of the activity

and the guests may be disturbing to some. This greatly depends upon the type of special guests and the clients in your group.

5. **Use your senses.** Look around you and see all the various objects of interest (i.e., different colors, different shapes, different sizes, etc.). Utilize a range of any particular category (e.g., leaves, rocks, tree bark, flowers, etc.). Use your other senses in the same way and explore the world much like a child does. Bring in objects to feel, see, smell, hear, and taste. Discuss and experience. Thinking back to childhood may be a helpful way to look at things. Remember how even the littlest things were intriguing? Present items to the clients with the same intrigue.

6. **Make your group room or meeting place more attractive and stimulating.** Use the following materials and ideas.

A large welcome sign

Corkboard for posting artwork, news items, etc.

Large calendar for displaying birthdays and holidays

Seasonal room decorations

Large map of the United States where each person's birth place can be
    shown with a pin and paper marker

Name tags for each person, including staff

Shelves for personal belongings

Microphone and amplifier

Remember, the group leader is one of the most important elements in making any activity you generate into a GREAT ACTIVITY!